CONTEMPORARY DETAILS

CONTEMPORARY DETAILS

NONIE NIESEWAND

MITCHELL BEAZLEY

CONTEMPORARY DETAILS
by Nonie Niesewand

First published in Great Britain in 1992
by Mitchell Beazley,
an imprint of Octopus Publishing Group Ltd,
Michelin House, 81 Fulham Road,
London SW3 6RB

Reprinted 1995, 1996, 1997, 1998, 1999 (with revisions)

Design Director **Jacqui Small**
Executive Editor **Judith More**
Design **Town Group Consultancy Ltd**
Editors **Jonathan Hilton, John Wainwright**
Editorial Assistants **Jaspal Bhangra, Catherine Smith**
Production **Ted Timberlake**

The publishers will be grateful for any information that will assist them in keeping
future editions up to date. Although all reasonable care has been taken in the
preparation of this book, neither the publishers nor the compilers can accept any
liability for any consequence arising from the use thereof, or the
information contained therein.

A CIP catalogue record for this book is available from the British Library

ISBN 0 85533 947 0

Set in Trade Gothic Bold Condensed, Trade Gothic Light and Garamond 3 Italic
by Town Group Consultancy Ltd, London W3
Colour reproduction by Scantrans Pte Ltd, Singapore

Printed in China by Toppan Printing Co., (HK.) Ltd.

Page 1 Steel railings punctuate a mezzanine balcony in a conversion of a redundant power station into a recording studio by Julian Powell-Tuck.
Page 2 & 3 Wooden boards, white walls and glazed screens are the sparest of contemporary details in an interior by the former partnership of Claudio Silvestrin and John Pawson.
Right Venetian blinds filter light across the mezzanine floor in a house by David Wild.

Contents

Introduction

The first international guide to contemporary details is an invaluable source of ideas and innovative products for anyone interested in 20th-century interior design. Contemporary Details presents design innovations and technological developments that have made it into the mass market because of their usefulness and good looks. Form follows function in designs for the clean-cut, contoured interiors of today, where period pieces are as out of place as a Victorian fireplace aboard a space shuttle. This is a book for homeowners who want to live in the present and who look forward to the future. It is not the book for people who wish to disguise their radiators with trelliswork or hide their televisions under skirted tablecloths, or for those who believe the builders left early if they do not see mouldings on every wall. Intensive sleuthwork among the top manufacturers in Europe, the United States and Japan reveals patented inventions: armourplated

security doors that masquerade as friendly tongue-and-grooved front doors, door handles that can store both daylight and artificial light to glow in the dark, the high-heat

ceramics pioneered by microwave cookery transformed into slimline, wall-mounted heater panels or sculpted into geometric firebricks for smokeless fires. The original and unusual ideas on show include an oven with a curved concave front that turns corners gracefully, slimline ceiling-mounted loudspeakers built into acoustic tiles in bathrooms to beam music in while showering, battens profiled like dado rails that hide wall-mounted tube lighting to delineate stairs with a lit handrail and photo-sensitive lights that turn on when people enter the room. Less obvious in their technological attraction, but no less innovative, are products like energy-conscious window blinds that store sunlight and release it during the night to warm the glazed areas or energy-conscious ovens that steam cook as well as convection fan heat.

Innovations in manufacturing bring back hand-made techniques that are in reality machine-cut and mass-produced. Mosaic tiles or parquet patterns arrive on site already

Previous pages
Materials used for fixtures and fittings in John Young's apartment display the influence of industrial design on domestic architecture.
1 David Wild uses details built to last: metal rails, granite windowsills, wooden flooring and a stainless steel chimney flue.
2 Pared-down kitchens are essential in small city homes, like this town house by Pierre d'Avoine. Many appliance manufacturers offer slimline fittings for limited space.
3 Andrée Putman renovated the interior of Le Corbusier's Villa Turque as a machine for living, in the spirit of its architect.

4

assembled, pasted onto templates, to fit geometric con-figurations. Art is translated into wall-to-wall carpet with the newest Timbrelle acrylic yarns, so finely tuned to carpet weaving that artists' and architects' artwork can be reproduced accurately by the metre and less expensively than linoleum flooring. Tooling up a factory to make new

5

products means they are effec-tively marketed worldwide, and consequently less expensive than one-offs or customized finishes; although Contemporary Details also examines these specialist

areas so popular with contemporary interior designers. There is nothing mechanical about all this mass production. Rather, a lot of thoughtful comment about the expressive new designs that shows how functional form can be good-looking. Take the ordinary door handle as an example, and note the comments of designer Jasper Morrison: "Few products are so closely involved with architecture as the door handle. As soon as it is fixed it becomes part of the building

6

7

and will have an influence on how the building works." Yet this attitude is not accompanied by grandiose flourishes: "If the user is aware of the handle every time the door opens, something is wrong." So, containing a place for the forefinger, the thumb, and the convex arch, these door handles are high-touch, rather than high-tech. Style does not take second place to technological innovations: there are traditional kitchen white goods coloured black with simple to follow electronic controls; thermally insulated aluminium window frames clad with "Clima" wooden façades; ceramic-clad stoves in the traditional wood-burning shape fired and wired for top-heat gas,

8

and triangular baths that tuck into corners while offering whirlpool massage techniques.

The story of modern fittings dates from the mid-19th century as products began to be made in factories by machines, instead of by hand. As the bentwood café chair began to roll off the assembly line at the steam-pressed timber

4 Lighting is the interior designer's most exciting tool – from built-in wall, floor and ceiling background lights to theatrical spots that pivot and move to decorative task lighting, uplights and modern chandeliers. Tadao Ando employs all of these in his sparse interiors.
5 Extendable chromed mirrors and marble surfaces are typical of the minimal style of John Pawson.
6 David Chipperfield combines different flooring materials – slate, granite, wood – to demarcate areas of an open-plan house.
7 Arata Isozaki's design for an ascent to a bunk-like sleeping area frees floor space.
8 A spider's web of metal is strung together for a dramatic staircase by Eva Jiricna.

Right Philippe Starck's designs for the Royalton Hotel, New York are now available for the domestic market. The "Royalton" collection's signature horn motif appears as lights, door handles, vases, fenders and even fire tongs.

yards of Thonet, the era of the artisan came to an end. The cabinetmaker, stonemason and gilder rapidly found their skills obsolete as technology developed in response to scientific discovery. By the 1880s, while machines continued to mass-produce furniture and fixtures, an aesthetic revolt was brewing, led by the Arts and Crafts movement in Britain but quickly taken up elsewhere in Europe and in North America. Designers wanted a return to the deliberate craftsmanship and simple design of the Middle Ages, with stained-glass door panels recalling ecclesiastical windows and giant pewter hinges replacing Victorian brass fittings. English artist and social reformer William Morris pontificated on simplicity, fine craftsmanship and the belief that good design should be available to all, regardless of their social standing. His sentiments were admirable but doomed to failure – in a machine age, any solutions to the problem of machine aesthetics must work with, not against, the machine.

One offshoot of the movement was Art Nouveau, which drew its inspiration from Nature. Samuel Bing's Paris shop, La Maison de l'Art Nouveau, opened in 1895, spearheaded the style with Tiffany glass, Beardsley posters and Lalique jewellery in room settings by Henry van de Velde. The movement incurred Le Corbusier's epitaph: "an intolerable period, Art Nouveau – a time of crushing bourgeois values sunk in materialism bedecked with mechanical decorations." In Vienna, by contrast, designers confronted the dilemma of the machine age head on. "To each time its art, to each art its freedom" was carved above the door to the Secessionist Gallery where Adolf Loos and Josef Hoffmann led a designer protest against the pompous, historicist Ringestrasse

style of the Neoclassicists. Hoffmann's style evolved in a geometric and structural direction and his door handles and lights made for the Palais Stoclet in Brussels in 1905 – a landmark of residential modern architecture – are still in production.

In Germany, the School of Arts and Crafts changed its name to the Bauhaus (literally "building house") in 1919, when Walter Gropius, the father of Modernism, became its new director. Adopting the American architect Louis Sullivan's principle "form follows function", the immensely influential Bauhaus group aimed for high-quality machine production, bringing industry and art together to create prototypes for mass consumption. New techniques and materials made this possible, and Bauhaus members went on to pioneer a series of world firsts, from the cantilevered chair to the transparent armchair and shelf. When Le Corbusier applied the same principle to domestic architecture, describing the home as a machine for living, the worldwide reign of modern style had begun.

Between the world wars another style, known as Art Deco or French Moderne, also flourished. The hit of the 1925 l'Exposition des Arts Decoratifs in Paris, Art Deco was at first modernistic rather than historical in its inspiration. Plastic, shagreen, tinted and frosted glass were used for interior fittings and Jacques-Emile Ruhlman and Pierre Chareau came up with neat solutions to seating and storage. However, in the 1930s Deco designers borrowed from pop culture as well as Bauhaus. The iconography of transport, jazz and the movies were central to Art Deco, but when excitement about the exploration of King Tutankhamen's tomb led to the adoption of sun-ray motifs and other

symbols derived from Egyptian papyrus scrolls, the sheer geometry of the style made it difficult to clasp a door handle, let alone turn it.

In the early 1940s came organic curves from Scandinavia and the Finnish architect Alvar Aalto. Simple but bold fabrics, curvaceous glass, bentwood simplicity and sleek, stylish steel bath and kitchen taps and mixers are still associated with this movement.

Meanwhile, in Italy a rationalist organization called Gruppo 7, founded by Guiseppe Terragni, designed structures which mirrored the simplicity of form pioneered by Alvar Aalto, with exposed new brick, timbered beams and the lengthy glass panels that larger kilns could now produce. The exposed technical elements – for heat and light – were a forerunner of Minimalism in the 1970s.

The Case Study House experiment which Ray and Charles Eames conducted at the Cranbrook Academy in the United States in 1948 mixed materials in a thoroughly Modern aesthetic in order to construct an inexpensive liveable house out of standard factory parts. Wood and leather took on shapes like aeroplane wings; the pressing and moulding techniques of the aeronautical industry combined to make furnishings which stacked, flexed, folded and rolled.

All over the world, mid-century modernism evolved against a background of interior stone walls or mosaic tiles, with terrazzo floors replicated in linoleum, lit by recessed lighting, or three-in-a-row hanging lamps, while spindly legged furniture sat on brushed-pile rugs in neon colours and the television took pride of place.

Alongside the flowering of a counter-culture in the 1960s came a loosening-up of form, encouraged by the fluid new materials – moulded plastic, fibreglass and wire mesh. The Italians began to develop their sleek modern style. There was less wood around and new lamp sources, primary colours and moulded forms became important features. After such exuberance, the Minimalism of the 1970s was inevitable. Designers worked with attenuated lines, making things smaller, lighter and more moveable as they explored materials like carbon fibre. Pressed metal came into its own for stair treads and chair supports, its industrial punch-card imagery relating to the new high-tech look as cladding was ripped away and the inner organs of a building – its air-conditioning and heating, its stairs and elevators – became adornment on the outside.

As the pendulum swung again, 1980s designers turned their attention to volume and mass under the banner of a refined classic Modernism. A more playful pop imagery was allowed. Suddenly surface finish was all-important, with polychromatic glass panels, silk-panelled laminates and gilded accessories. Function is there in the detailing, but power-dressed as chairs sprout wings and fireplace fenders resemble Viking helmets. Robert Venturi ripped off Chippendale for Knoll International in two-dimensional form and Ettore Sottsass launched Memphis with its overscaled, colourful pieces.

While the Post-Modernists turned the skyline into backdrops for playschool, the 1980s also saw the emergence of the architectural interior designers – the graduate architects who have transformed the way we look at interiors. How do they differ from the decorators of old? One of them, Pierre d'Avoine, sums it up like this: "The interior designer plays with spaces, the decorator with camouflages."

Right Every detail in Sir Richard Rogers' London house – from tap to cupboard, balustrade to floor – has been chosen for ease of use and maintenance.

Good-looking, fashionable but lasting interiors are no longer a question of mouldings, dados, skirting, paint and flounce – all those age-old decorators' tricks of camouflage. They are functional, technologically advanced and, above all, they follow an idea that has been draughted along architectural principles. The innovative new young modern designers seek to throw out artifice; they prize the intrinsic integrity of the structural material. Throughout Contemporary Details examples of their work underline this approach. Their conversions within chapels, warehouses and office blocks have created homes out of space that had no relevance in today's world. And the result? Homes will never look the same again.

By using products designed to make life more comfortable and more leisurely, the products themselves have come to represent not a style, but an attitude. Set in the context of vernacular materials – corrugated metal panels, steel girder steps, plywood walls and ceilings of wavy plastic, flake-board and corrugated carport aluminium – contemporary detailing allows for individual expression.

Products reflect the way in which we want to live today, with far-sighted views, generous spaces and lyrical light. British architect Julian Powell-Tuck believes that: "Attitudes reflect the fact that there are more women at work than before." So the latest appliances ranged in kitchens can do most things, and they have provoked "a new break-down of space within the home, with one long room combining dining, cooking and living, and clusters of cells off it for study, sleep, bathing."

The architectural legacy of the Modernists has altered forever the shape and purpose of the home and its new practitioners value honesty, simplicity and integrity. After all, the elaborate swags and festoons that are still reproduced from "retro" decorators from 100-year old pattern books were devised when drapes were the only way of making a house draughtproof.

The challenges for today's designers include how to heat the space efficiently, how to light it without cords and how to climb a level without taking out great chunks of the room in what Pierre d'Avoine calls "B-movie architecture". Indeed, with property prices in cities making floorspace so expensive, the question is, quite simply, how to save space. Market research has encouraged manufacturers to produce slimline kitchen appliances, for example, that suit the small kitchens and families in today's cities. And with social awareness one of the givens, the solutions have to recognize our anxiety about the environment.

Every decade of the 20th century has brought greater mobility and increased income to the industrialized world as a whole, and the ideals expressed by William Morris at the turn of the century are a little closer to being realized. "Good design for all," is the favourite maxim of Philippe Starck, France's most celebrated architect/interior designer. A commission from President Mitterrand in 1978 to design a private apartment at the Champs Elysées Palace propelled him far ahead of the mainstream matte-black design crowd, but Starck still cites as the best example of contemporary design his pack-flat furniture at low prices for the mail-order catalogue company, Trois Suisses. "Functional, accessible, appropriate" is the criterion upon which all the stylish innovations shown in Contemporary Details are judged.

Walls & Ceilings

Previous page
Architect Steven Holl's interiors reflect his fascination with materials. Here, he contrasts blue-stained wooden storage fronts with the milky opalescence of perspex shielding the light tubes.

1 Glass panels allow light to filter through. This "Polifemo" glass tile by R. Lucadamo for MITO has, additionally, the chromatic variation that makes for an interestingly textured surface.

The spaces within which interior designers prefer to work all tend to have certain characteristics in common: unbroken, long expanses uninterrupted by openings and space-inhibiting walls. Gallery space is the most enviable, and many architects working on domestic interiors strive toward a "flow of space" by removing walls. To achieve this, load-bearing internal walls are replaced by the modern "rafters" that dissect ceilings – the reinforced steel joist (RSJ). The additional space created by this simple ploy often means that the dividing walls become more shapely as architects rethink the linear grid upon which so much of modern box housing was developed. Planes and angles and sinuous wavy lines insinuate their way into interiors, just as they did at the start of the 20th century with Frank Lloyd Wright's exploration of "organic" architecture in the vernacular. Wright threw out this challenge: "Americans, in seeking culture, could not accept that posts and beams could be thrown away in favour of folding or

2

2 Modern architects favour the removal of boxed-in walls to create the feeling of free space. In their place, they tend to prefer sliding partitions that can be positioned to seal off an area when needed, or slid back to reveal an uninterrupted expanse. In his own home, architect Sir Richard Rogers used industrial roller systems, grooved and tracked, to clamp opaque glass partition walls in place.

3

3 Rooms seen only in artificial light, like the busy professional's drawing room and study, warrant dramatic wall treatments which might appear bold or even shrill in the harsh light of day. Malcolm Last painted the walls in this jazz club in pink and eau-de-nil, which transform to purple and chartreuse under night-time lighting.

4 Tadao Ando's trademark is his use of poured concrete walls. Unadorned, they represent the perfect foil for this Japanese architect's reinterpretation in modern glass of traditional shojis – translucent floor-to-ceiling panels, which allow walls to become doors. Bare concrete, coarse-seamed and studded with holes at regular intervals, becomes a canvas for evolving light patterns as the sun strikes the walls.

5 Clearly, East meets West in these concrete stud wall panels in David Chipperfield's offices. Chipperfield enjoys contrasts, of concrete with stainless steel or marble, for example. He will also set painted steel frames filled with panels of sand-blasted glass into areas of concrete wall.

4

5

19

1 & 2 These examples of John Pawson's work reveal something of his challenge to modernism. Slender white walls (above) flanking the stairs show how in this passageway nothing interrupts the flow. In his monolithic wall (above right), slab-like partitions hover over the floor, while a slender column appears to support the ceiling in an otherwise empty space.

3 In this David Wild interior the ridged steel ceiling undulates sinuously across the room to bring unity to this dining space, in which the cantilevered Bauhaus chairs help to replicate that directional flow.

2

4 Normally the atrium is the widest glazed opening in a building, but Frank Fitzgibbons reverses this order with a monumental ascent using massive wall volumes that narrow and thin toward the top, while the tubular rails and guards emphasize the stages of the ascent.

5 Ron Brinkers uses the adobe approach in this curvaceous wall, which appears to end in a triangular dovetail at the corner. This is emphasized below by a triangular plaster shelf. Slender ceiling-to-floor glass panels enhance the dimensions of the plasterwork walls.

movable planes, nor that organic architecture could derive from the tall grass of the mid-western prairies."

It was Frank Lloyd Wright who challenged the traditional subdivision of the home into separate rooms. In his houses built around Chicago in the first decade of the 20th century, each space was linked to and integrated with the landscape outside, as walls made way for the large, unbroken living room, with cells for bedrooms, studies and bathrooms fringing it. Modernism, that catch-all name for a panoply of styles since the Industrial Revolution, has seen a shift from the early moderne of Le Corbusier and the Bauhaus school of the late 1920s and 30s to the frankly flamboyant façades and wall finishes of the post-modern school, to the new simplicity of the late-modern movement. From glass to gloss to gleam in 20-year periods, the shift has come about through an interest in materials.

Fascinating materials are in use today: light-sensitive filters like camera lenses, opening and closing according to light levels, with which the French architect Jean Nouvel fronted his Arab

4

8, 9, 10 & 11 Id-Ekor specializes in wallcoverings. Their "Sajade" material is made from cotton, mineral and plant fibres. A special water-proofing solution is available.

8

9

10

5

13 Charles Rutherfoord blocked out a ziggurat basement wall with this softly flowing one to house a flue and slate hearth, echoing the shape of the piano to be housed in the room. To emphasize the theatricality of the effect, he rubbed red pigments into the polished plaster.

12 "Plastline" from Id-Ekor, is a marble and acrylo-synthetic wall-covering that is resistant to temperature change and abrasion. It also keeps out damp.

11

6 The novel use of modern building materials, usually clad with plaster, serves, like exposed beams, to structurally adorn this interior. RSJs inverted at right-angles delineate the change of wall direction and demarcate the unusual skirting boards. Even the door jamb is a solid pillar of rough-hewn stone, and the flooring changes from boards to slate.

12

6

7 Charles Rutherfoord describes himself as an architect/designer. Unclad, the macho materials of the building site become surfaces for his interiors. As a theatrical touch, pigments were rubbed into the panels, which, with the well of light above, have a surface play of light and shadow in steely pewter.

7

Institute building in Paris; reflective glass that becomes transparent when the lights are turned on at night to reveal the interior. In his vision of the future of London in the year 2066, the British architect Nigel Coates predicts that by the middle of the 21st century buildings will be a series of pods or cells created from DNA membranes that slide into load-bearing frameworks to form partitions that vary space according to need.

Although Coates propels science-fiction materials into his prediction, the principle of creating rooms within rooms using mass-produced components already exists. Partition walls, a trunking system of flooring that includes raised platforms, and ceiling panels, all of which interlock, are features of some current buildings. The ability of steel frames to span large distances without support means that the wall can be reduced to a mere in-fill between structural elements, providing thermal and acoustic insulation. How curiously lacking in imagination it makes the published pronouncements in Vogue in 1961 in an article entitled "Fashions in

13

1 The fashionable decade for paint finishes, the 1980s, launched many methods of paint application, including period-style rag rolling, scumbling and sponging finishes. As the 20th century concludes, there are new applications that involve metallic finishes and spray-gunning. Ingrid Stegmann is among the many con-temporary designers applying specialist finishes such as this one, which involves layers of metallic bronzes shot with gold

2 The citric yellow of Vico Magistretti's "Sinbad" sofas, inspired, he claims, by horse blankets, is sharpened by the soft swirls of paint rubbed on the walls. This is allowed to dry before other colours are sponged over it. The result is reminiscent of vellum papers.

3 Abet Laminate has coloured patterns running like geological seams through the material. Abet's "Serifragia" swatches for wall finishes, shown here, are popular with architects. Alessandro Mendini specified Abet Laminates for the exterior of the Groningen Museum in Holland, with interiors designed by Frank Stella, Philippe Starck and Michele de Lucchi.

4 Charles Rutherfoord lowered a ceiling in a narrow room with curved plywood panels. Special paint effects enhance the walls.

5 A wild effect here from Ingrid Stegmann, creating a sunset of colours illuminated with flashes of gold. This artist employs a team of craftsmen and women to apply gilded finishes. These owe nothing to mannerist fancies of another era, which is why you see them only in contemporary interiors as a background to modern furniture and lights.

6

6 A column is given an etched relief with the dado panels in Abet's "Straticolor" laminate, which, when engraved, shows another colour beneath the original finish.

7

7 The cornice, a narrow, glazed vertical strip above coloured walls, with a ridged steel ceiling apparently supported on a single column, brings light from every aspect into architect David Wild's own house

8 Charles Rutherfoord uses a collage of old manuscript papers and polished plaster to achieve this abstract art wall. Specialist decorators and designers, Nobby Clark and Partners, achieve many of the special effects for Rutherfoord.

9

Living" that recorded the decorator Esteban Cerda at Green & Abbott as saying:

"Even in an empty room, wallpaper transforms the walls from a mere architectural entity into something new." In the modern interior, architects use light, the architectural fourth dimension, to highlight walls and thus reduce their apparent mass and volume. The simple trick of recessing fluorescent lights just above the floor and below the ceiling makes solid walls appear to float on a sea of light. So, too, does recessing the plaster at skirting board level, and then painting a dark strip in the recess. This creates the illusion of the floorboards slipping away beneath the walls and thus contributes to the sense of weightlessness.

Lights also affect ceiling plans, since low-voltage lighting requires transformers. These are hidden in the ceiling, which is lowered and insulated to muffle noise and save energy. Dotted with prismatic recessed lights, the ceiling is at once freed from the single light bulb and shade suspended from a central ceiling rose.

10

11

8

9 A pillar, boxed in by plaster panels rubbed with pigments, and then deep etched and lined with metallic strips by Charles Rutherfoord creates a startling effect.

10 Architect Franklin D. Israel creates a cool, subterranean approach to the garden with scumbled blue walls that curvaceously lead to the glass exterior walls, and a low false ceiling adjoining at only one point.

11 Midnight blue rippled with gold-foil swirls creates a dramatic background in a modern room, illuminated by a single uplighter that plays light on the luminous paint finishes from Ingrid Stegmann.

23

1 Between an entrance with a leaning screen that inclines at an angle on steel rods, architect Stefano de Martino inserted two screens in the middle of the building before the gable-end wall. De Martino uses screens to define different areas in more flexible ways than solid walls would.

4

2 Artist Terry Flowers cast these screens in clear fibreglass, and they take their patinated shape from the mould. Architect Stefano de Martino has a great interest in the true nature of the products he uses, especially so in a world where so much is artifice.

3 In these offices, architect Stefano de Martino chose clear-glass walls. Within, sliding partition walls never really cut into the space like a barrier. Slicing through the false computer grid floor and into the concrete beneath means the partitions are freed from the building, and since they do not meet the ceiling they appear to float loosely in space.

The glass industry has provided archi-tects with new ways to optimize natural light, from glass that changes its opaqueness as the light intensity varies, to frosted glass blocks that transmit filtered light in attractive ways. When it became possible in the 1950s to build large, frameless glass walls, glass lost its horticultural associations and be-came a symbol of the clean, fresh lines of modernity.

Mies van der Rohe, who produced an idealized version of the "house without walls" for the Barcelona exhibition in 1929, perfected his style by 1959, at Farnsworth House. Here he used large sheets of clear glass as walls to make the entire structure invisible in effect. For more solid structures, the harmony of unbroken wall space is refined with spray-gun-lacquered finishes designed to reflect light or, in kitchens and

4 All the colours of the sea and sky can be seen in these glass tiles from the Venetian glass blowers A.V. Mazzega, designed by Massimo Rioda.

5 Glass bricks have been developed by Pilkington to create large wall spaces in the nominal sizes of tiles that include the joint width. Gwathmey Siegel here lines up a full panel of glass bricks with a view to an inner courtyard.

6

6 A submarine viewing window set into a steel hatch door is flanked with glazed bricks in architect Eva Jiricna's own apartment.

7 Framing glass bricks with panels or matte-black produces a grid-like formality, as architect Jo Crepain realizes. Frames can exaggerate the horizontal or vertical – omitting them effectively "knocks-back", visually, a glazed brick section without delineating each brick.

8, 9 & 10 The "Heroes" collection from Mito, designed by Fraboni, uses layers of glass moulded in relief to suggest the effects of unpeeling, fracture, splinter and curl. The designs here are "Tebe" (far right), "Itaca" (above right) and "Cartago" (below right).

11 Armstrong Associates use glass walls in this interior for architectural fittings company Elementor. The advantage of glass is that the passage of light through a building is not impeded by partitions. Technological advances in the manufacture of glass, with larger sheets being produced, and in fittings (see picture **12**), have given today's architects more flexibility in the use of glass for walls.

12 Pilkington's wall planar structural glazing system is one of the most versatile wall clamps available. Flexible silicone-sealed joints between panels provide a structurally glazed envelope without frames or mullions.

bathrooms, panelling of tiles or veneers of marble, granite or slate.

Fashions in tiling move from the most obvious contrasts, such as black gloss with white grouting, to the more subtle matte tiles in tiny squares that achieve the effect of a mosaic. You can achieve a subtle sheen from concrete walls, unadorned but for dry powder paint rubbed into the mixture before application. This appeals to those impressed by the patina of age on such a modern material.

While coloured walls work like an abstract painting in some instances (Jean Michel Frank's colourful early Art Deco interior in Paris sported one pink, one pale-blue, one sea-green, and one yellow wall), pattern has been the decorator's preferred choice. But bold backgrounds are back in business, with patterned laminate panels by Abet in

1 Corrugated aluminium on castors makes up this innovative panelled screen. Jacques Borris creates his designs on the "backs of envelopes" and then finds people willing to produce them.

2 Twenty square tiles make up this screen, called "Paravent", in the Mito collection. The screen can be placed wherever needed, as a room divider or window screen.

3 & 4 With this collection of glass, Dimensione Fuoco glamorizes an ancient craft. "Notte" (left) and "Giardino" (right) were designed by architects Afra and Tobia Scarpa in a limited series of ten pieces and are set into leaded panels.

5 Open-plan living has never been the same since architect Michael Hopkins revolutionized building practices with his own

house that has no conventional walls. The exterior walls are glass and room dividers throughout, except for the minimum of rigid wall to carry bathroom and kitchen plumbing, are Venetian blinds from Faber.

6 This wall system of coloured luminous listels, "Colora", is by Carlo A. Urbinati Ricci and Alessandro Vecchiato for Foscarini. Its mounts enable the glass slats to be changed to modify the composition.

7 A four-panelled screen effectively blocks out one of the glass walls facing the garden in a house by Franklin D. Israel.

Japanese interiors traditionally use shoji screens – translucent paper "walls" in a wooden frame – to divide up space. The Japanese theme inspired this bedroom in America, by architect Gwathmey Siegel, where even the bed is a simple futon on the floor.

11 Pierre d'Avoine created six small houses that manage to look light and open. The kitchen folds away behind a screen, stairs to the galleried upper floor are hidden, and the low ceiling height beneath the gallery and on the upper floor are all part of a clever juggling with space.

8 A thin, opaque sliding screen by architects John Pawson and Claudio Silvestrin serves to pace the space differently, without severance or intrusion.

9 The heavily ornamented panelled screen of Piero Fornasetti's "Pompiana" reproduces classical architectural elements. Despite its size, it can easily be moved about on its industrial castors.

Italy, who gave the Italian maestro Ettore Sottsass Jnr the opportunity to colour them in, and then pioneered a way of diffusing light through the panels in a collection known as "Diafos".

It was Sottsass who introduced at the Museum of Modern Art in New York in 1972 his "Habitat", a structure made up of movable blocks, each of which had a different function. All of the blocks could be opened, closed, packaged, even warehoused, and "Habitat" certainly did away with the concept of conventional load-bearing walls as we know them.

The architect Alessandro Mendini, speaking of his intentions for both interior and exterior walls for his Groningen Museum in Holland, declares his love for artistry in assembling colour and pattern across such large surfaces: "Brick, aluminium, concrete and laminates, coloured delicately in pale blue, ochre, yellow and pink, gold and silver combine in an unusual way reminiscent of cubism."

Materials more often associated with design and sculpture rather than architecture, such as laminates,

12 From Zanotta, this three-fold screen "Paramenta" by De Pas, d'Urbino and Lomazzi, stands on four feet. Its central panel has irregular wavy fine lines, replicating the same waves on the flanking pair.

13 Inlaid marquetry fans proclaim the Spanish origins of "Abanicos" as boldly as the traditional Valencian cabinetry on the six-panelled screen, by Jaime Tresserra Clapes.

1 The Fendi collection of double-fired wall tiles, "Astrologia", draws its inspiration from the 12 constellations of the Zodiac.

polychromatic silk-screened panelling, mosaics and aluminium, are becoming decorative wall claddings.

Modernists, who would not think to give house room to those ornamental mouldings that are so often produced today in polystyrene, are using "Cornice", a design by two Spaniards, Ramon Bigas and Pep Sant, since these cornices work as a contemporary detail rather than as a crown running along the top of a wall.

Their system of architectural mouldings is designed like a segment of cylindrical tubing in which there are lights, either metal-halide or fluorescent types, installed within its slim profile, as well as glass shelving. Thus, it does multiple duty in different areas of the home: as a stair rail following the line of the staircase; as an architectural feature at dado rail or cornice height; or as a source of illumination for bathroom storage.

2 Modular wood wall and ceiling panels by Tilo can be positioned and coloured to influence optically the proportions of rooms. The finishes available include oak, antique oak, ash, mahogany, beech, teak, cherry (shown here), larch, spruce and pine.

3 Moulded borders by Orac Decor create a classical wall finish. The mouldings are polyurethaned, lightweight and simple to glue in place.
4 The "Domino" system from Glass Design uses three acid-etched patterns in a panel of nine sheets of reflective glass.

5 Innovative and brilliant in concept, the "Cornice" is a multi-purpose system of mouldings designed by Bigas and Sant.

6 Within this ceiling from Svedbergs are built-in hi-fi speakers, waterproofed and ready to connect to your stereo system. Also available are low-voltage light tiles with four halogen lights, complete with transformer.
7 The sunray effect ceiling in ash wood panelling from Tilo accentuates a particular area and so helps to create rooms within rooms – such as this library introduced to a drawing room.

8 A narrow space carved out of a landing for an office in a mews house by Peter Wilson, displays wood panels arranged like a chequerboard according to the grain of the veneer. And a scooped billow of a ceiling, painted orange, echoes in its grandiose curves the desk designed by Royal College of Art Professor Floris van den Broeke.

9

10

9 Ship-like wooden panels cover a curved corridor wall in a house by Peter Wilson. **10** Orac Decor make medallions, cornice and panel mouldings, corners, columns, capitals and plinths to dramatize pedestrian walls and ceilings. Their high-density polyure-thane mouldings easily adhere to surfaces, as in this Art Deco revival-ist room, where a dado rail with two columns and white mouldings create ziggurat wall panels to frame pictures.

1, 2 & 3 Frost- and skid-resistant paviors from Blockleys would make unusual textured facings for walls. The "Rope" pattern pavior (**2**) was specially commissioned; patterned bricks can be designed and fired to order. "Corduroy" directional guidance paviors (**1** and **3**) are graphically ribbed.

4 Blockleys' "Tactile" paviors can be used for walls although they were designed to be installed at traffic crossing points as a valuable aid to the blind.

5 A pre-cast, matte-grey concrete panel system on the walls of Tadao Ando's house is complemented by polished concrete panels on the ceiling, the latter designed to reflect natural light from the large window down into the room.

6 Contemporary designers like Ron Resik use brick for interior as well as exterior walls. Some build walls of brick, while others face concrete on breeze-block in slim brick-tiles.

8

9

10

8, 9 & 10 Facing bricks from Blockleys – "Saffron Yellow, Mellow Grain" (top), "Black Mixture, Wrekin Briar" (above left) and "X Mixture, Wirecut" (above right) – are suitable for interior and

exterior use because they are frost-resistant and subject to low/nil efflorescence and low water absorption.

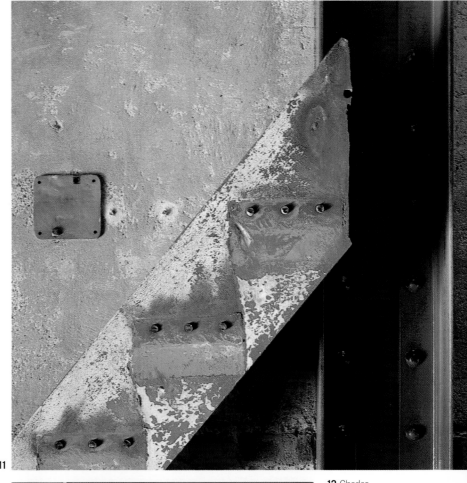

11

7 & 11 Original industrial surfaces are stripped back and left in the raw in a domestic conversion of a power station by architect Gary Cunningham.

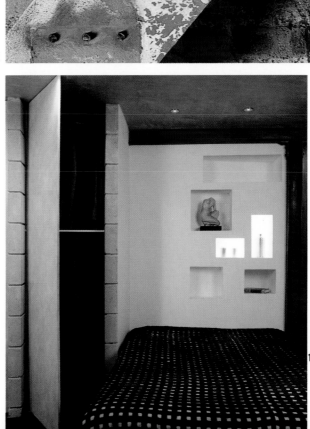

12

12 Charles Rutherfoord has built small alcoves into a bedroom wall to provide useful display and storage areas in a confined space.

1, 2 & 3 "Metropolis" from Gianfranco Salvi's "Reflections of Italy Collection" are embossed vinyl wallcoverings.

1

2

3

4 "Pergamena Intarsio" from Riflessitaliani sets geometric patterns of hand-made parchment into washable vinyl with a soft, velvety finish. Gianfranco Salvi developed "Intarsio" from his "Karta Pergamena" paper (see **9**) to create a version with wider applications.

4

5 From the "Heavy Metal" collection by Riflessitaliani, "Pyramid" is a metallic finish vinyl. These deeply embossed wallcoverings have substantial acoustical qualities.

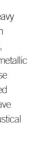

5

6 For "Graniti", Riflessitaliani have developed a special manufacturing method to obtain a wallpaper that is comparable to real granite. It can be used on walls that are not suitable for the weight of granite facing.

6

7

8

7 & 8 "Rivet" is a metallic vinyl wallcovering from the "Heavy Metal" collection by Riflessitaliani. In renovation work, simulated metal finishes pose none of the earthing problems for electrical outlets that real metal would bring.

9 Riflessitaliani is renowned for its "Karta Pergamena" collection of flame-resistant hand-painted papers in 21 different shades. The most striking are dusted with pure gold and silver. The product is also manufactured as a "Museum" floor tile by saturating it in melamine and backing it with PVC.

9

Floors

There is no quicker way to direct attention to one part of a room than by covering it with pattern. Long ago, Venetians used bold pattern on the floor of every interior, with mosaics made from marble and terrazzo, while the Spanish used Moorish tiles in turquoise and orange to delineate the courtyard at the heart of their houses. In softer materials, the French spun delicious sherbet colours like lime and raspberry in the flora and fauna carpets of Aubusson; while in Brussels, weavers stretched Gobelin tapestries into enormous hunting scenes. The English perfected the art of needlepoint, the Moslems worldwide used hand-stitching and disciplined geometrics to establish regional variations, while in Holland, the patterned oiled floorcloth became fashionable. Bokhara kilims, Berber rugs from the Sahara, dhurries in Indian cotton woven in stripes, Peruvian woven rugs and Mexican serapes – all these names read like a travel guide and conjure up the magic carpets of fable while offering colour and pattern underfoot.

Previous page Art by the yard/metre is now available from famous artists and architects at affordable prices from Vorwerk carpets. The carpets closely resemble the originals in colour, line, brushstrokes and shading. This "Dialog 2" design is by graphic designer Milton Glaser.

1 A glazed tile in monochrome greys with a bark-like relief is by Rex Ceramiche with Trussardi in Italy.
2 From the "Grofisimi" collection comes "Negro" by Azuvi – a tile veined like marble. Its single-fired glaze gives it a textured effect, though smooth-surfaced.

3 Limited edition hand-knotted carpets with a pure wool warp on a cotton weft are the work of young artists and famous designers for Elio Palmisano. Beppe Caturegli's "Magdalena" has dance steps in a galaxy of colour. Processing methods have been perfected with the aid of advanced craft technologies.

4

5 The "Marie Antoinette" pattern on hardwood flooring from Rowi Parket is laid on foam underlay to help absorb sound. Interchangeable square boards allow designers to create unique, customized patterns and achieve a variety of dramatic effects.

4 A King Kong view of London's Thames is on show from a penthouse apartment by architect John Young. Its rooftop steel walkways to the terrace and circular, reinforced opaque-glass inlets visually enhance the shipdeck image while allowing portholes of light to filter through to the floors below.

6 Vinyl flooring replicates any hardwood or stone surface. In their "Perspectives" collection, Amtico's "Alabaster SM 6", with green strips and "Florentine NM 7" borders, looks handcrafted.

7 Another Vorwerk carpet, this design is by artist Gerhard Richter and repeats his 1970s paintings in which he experiments with paint manufacturers' colour cards.

5 Oiled beech wood, less than 1 inch (22 mm) thin, from Junckers is factory-sealed for stain resistance, which makes it suitable for use in kitchens. Other wooden floorings with an oiled finish that are available from Junckers include ash, elm and oak.

6 An acoustically sound maple floor re-placed concrete slabs in a conversion of an electricity generator plant for a music lover. In the recital room, adjustable shutters make the space virtually tuneable, or "acoustically bright" according to architect Gary Cunningham.

1 Conventional, medium-ash-brown strip floorboards have been inlaid with a cube of marbled mosaic using brown, white, black and grey stone to break up a long run of regular flooring in this house by Roberto Serino.

2 Kentucky wood floors have hardwoods from lightest ash to darkest zebrawood. Felled in temperate zones, American hardwoods do not endanger the rain-forests. This medallion of mixed species is the focal point of the room.

3 The classic parquet pattern from Tarkett is only 7mm thick consisting of three layers of bonded veneers. The flooring is available in oak, ash, beech, birch, maple, red oak or fumed oak, and is laid in long strips.

4 This bleached beech floor whitened with pigments to shipdeck brightness is from Junckers, a producer of solid, hardwood flooring, whose specific-purpose floors include those made for gymnasiums.

In early American houses the lack of these rich materials led to the introduction of a new technique. The floor's surface was given a rubbing of coloured pigment as a background to stencilled patterns of holly leaves, birds and flowers. This decorative device has recently been revived in the modern interior as a way to introduce individuality to the room. Patterns are used either as a border or as a centrepiece.

It was the modernists who eventually laid the patterned floor to rest. Suddenly it became fashionable to have everything in plain board, cement or white tiles. Stone flagstones were permitted, according to the availability of locally found stone. Redbrick, that innovative building material of the 1960s, was also encouraged.

No wonder contemporary architects spend so much time—and clients' money—considering flooring, sometimes even designing it. Flooring is one of the largest expenses in a house, so choosing colours, textures and patterns is vital to the overall scheme. When planning flooring, an important point to bear in mind is the structure of the building

7 In a compact, city apartment, converted from a period house, architect Ron Brinkers simply stripped back and sanded the original beech floorboards. They provide a roughened contrast to a small, black wooden bridge that leads to the informal seating area.

9 A realistic wood strip floor in a bathroom is in fact vinyl from Amtico. This type of material will cope with condensation, always a problem in bathrooms, far better than the washed teak it copies. Accurate reproductions of 19 different woods are available in the range.

10 Red-oak, plank flooring from Rowi can be laid over an existing wooden floor or secured directly over concrete.

8 Maple parquet flooring from Tibbals Hartco in Tennessee is laid in slabs of horizontal and vertical strips to create an intricate flooring pattern simply.

itself. Solid concrete floors can support any type of flooring, but before laying something like quarry tiles on the average domestic wooden suspended floor you should seek advice on load-bearing from an expert.

When the looms at Axminster began to punch out wall-to-wall carpet, the world of uniformity began. Wall-to-wall beige or brown anonymity transformed hotels as far apart as Cairo and Kraków into identical clones of each other. And it became a domestic status symbol to have wall-to-wall carpeting everywhere at home, except the kitchen. In this room, flagstones by the yard became available in prepackaged vinyl that replicated hard flooring.

As the machine-age broadloom carpet asserted autumnal swirls wall-to-wall in rooms throughout the world, the contemporary designer left floors un-adorned. The result, a good timber floor or, in hot climates, a tiled one. Narrow, tongue-and-groove beechwood planks became the ubiquitous flooring favour-ite, together with matte-grey or white ceramic tiles for bathrooms. Sometimes the planks were laid diagonally to bring

1 Regular, hard-edged marble slabs have been laid diagonally, point to point, and then emphasized by cordoning off a large area with a fine, black travertine slip inlaid at an angle to the slabbed floor.
The effect, created by architect De Maria, is like a theatrically positioned rug thrown down on the floor. Marble is an exceptionally hard-wearing flooring material and, if well-sealed, impervious to staining. Cold to the touch, it is particularly suitable for homes in warm climates.

1

2

3

4

2, 3 & 4 What is commonly referred to as marble can, in fact, be precast material composed of marble chips bonded together with resin. This reconstituted material by Reed Harris is competitive in price, sold by the yard/metre as floor tiles, whereas true marble has been called the ultimate natural building material.

5 A narrow corridor could be dark and confining, but Ingo Maurer's trapeze lights strung merrily across doorways and ladder-like black and white marble and polyester resin floor tiles from MARBO give the space light as well as a dramatic, geometric configuration. A place to pause in rather than simply stride through, the design is by Studio Epton.

a crazy tilt to the room. Generous-width boards taken from old gymnasiums or from salvage yards often appear in the modern interior, their hand-hewn solidity and patina of age, their beautiful colour, sheen and grain making them matchless backgrounds.

Stained wood went through a revival in the 1970s. But when colour fashions change, sealer coats make such floors difficult to adapt. Painted wooden floors – using yacht deck paints – bring a certain nostalgic reminder of psychedelic colours, but it is fair to say that today's wooden floors are plainer. These are made from a softwood board, such as spruce, fir or pine, tongue-and-groove or butt-jointed; hardwood blocks in herringbone, basket or brick patterns; or the relatively inexpensive and flexible alternatives to solid wood – plywood and particle board (chipboard). Particle

5

6

6 Kirkstone is a light-sea-green volcanic stone obtained from England's Lake District. It is a popular, hard flooring now sold for export since new diamond-cutting processes make the stone quarriable.

board, made from shavings of wood chips set in a resin, can be laid in squares of varying thickness, sealed or unsealed. One of the undeniable facts of present-day hardwood floors is that they are not soundproofed, and it may therefore not be possible to use this material in an inner-city apartment.

If wood is not to your liking, then there are ceramic floor tiles, made of clay and fired at high temperatures, some with a nonslip finish. Tough, waterproof and impervious to staining, tiles can be heated under floor in colder climates, but really they are better suited to warmer countries. And the assertive patterning with which ceramic tiles are often decorated

7 Large-scale slate squares, shot with a narrow, triangular sliver of travertine here and there, act as pointers – to the exit, the furniture, the hearth – in this wittily appointed room, by designer and architect Philippe Starck, at the famous New York Royalton Hotel.

8 Conventional wisdom has it that for small floor areas you should keep to a continuous run of the same material underfoot. This is in the belief that changes of pattern and texture visually decrease the feeling of space. But architect David Chipperfield successfully changes direction – and materials – matching slivers of oak, slate and terrazzo on the floors in the kitchen and dining area of a compact house.

9, 10 & 11 "Quartz-line" floor covering by Id Ekor is made of coloured quartz pebbles set in resin. The resin-and-pebble mix is applied over an existing floor surface.

8

7

9

10

11

3, 4 & 5 Ceramic tiles from Matteo Baldini came in a range of rich and sophisticated finishes. "Impallinato" (above left) is by Michele de Lucchi; "Intrecciato" (above right) by Adolfo Natalini; and "Cinque" (left) by Andrea Branzi.

6 & 7 Little tesseras of marble and stone assembled in mosaics are now delivered in

1 Outlined in pale borders, with wide, grey concrete tiles to the wall, Sergio Puente uses patterned tiles like a rug, each tile featuring a diagonal cross in pastels, edged with a spiralling ribbon pattern, like a brushstroke hand-painted on the white ceramic glaze.

2 Andreas Weber uses large terracotta slabs grouted with pale grey cement in a regular pattern, which he then rearranges by placing a cream rug diagonally, as well as a low-slung platform bed at an angle to the floor tiles.

pre-cast patterns on backing papers with numbered joints for easy assembly on site. "Lux" (above) is in the series Gemmae by SICIS. "Nerone" (below) is a mosaic by SICIS made with marble and granite tesseras. The system reduces cutting and laying time.

makes them less popular than quarry tiles as a background flooring. Made from high-silica clay fired to an almost glass-like hardness, quarry tiles can be laid in square or rectangular slabs and are available in buff, amber, terracotta, dark blue or black.

A new hard-flooring product is a mosaic sold in patterns mounted on paper to make them easier to lay, or terrazzo marble chips, plain or coloured, set in cement and then ground to a smooth finish. Sandstone, yorkstone, granite and limestone slabs are also all hard-wearing flooring materials, and slate is an extremely popular, heathery coloured alternative, but it is really only suitable for use in a small room because of its high cost.

One of the interesting inventions of this century is without doubt the vinyl tile, or

8 "Scritture" by Ceramica Bardelli uses Grecian key motifs and Egyptian hieroglyphics to recreate a distinctive series of terracotta and black designer tiles. The complicated geometric designs match up with borders.

9 These white lime-stone flagstones – just over 1-inch (2.5-cm) thick to make them practical indoors – are from Paris Ceramics. The tiles can be cut into special shapes, though regular sizes are nearly 16 x 16 inches (40 x 40 cm). Their decorative patterns are highlighted by soft colour washes or special distressed finishes.

10 Within the confines of a severe, iconoclastic architecture, Andrew Holmes has laid an interesting motif on the floor. The design replicates the semi-circular window casting its light on that motif, and extends the pattern of light within a grid made up of black squares identical in size to the panes of glass in the window.

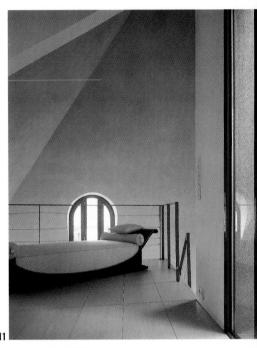

11

11 Cool, grey-stained wood laid in large panels resembles flagstones but has the advantage of being warm underfoot and suitable for laying over a wider range of floor surfaces.

12

12 Ceramica Sant'Agostino's "Tiffany" range of single-fired tiles are frost-resistant and strengthened with hard Stratos glaze, which is rich in aluminium and quartz.

13

13 Mexican terracotta tiles by Corres are marketed worldwide. The lime-rich Coahuila clay is recognizable by its mellow, pinky beige coloration.

FLOORS

1, 2 & 3 At this house Studio Epton has used the most sophisticated combinations of materials underfoot. Basic concrete is rubbed with pigment and inlaid with glass and wood patterns that are immaculately outlined in brass. Semi-circular glass swirls and splinters create a decorative scroll, while a stud of wood, like a bolt beside a sliver of opaque thickened glass, amusingly explores the idea of cabinet-makers' traditional joints. And a structure of fineline metal inserted in the concrete, in the manner of the Muslim countries' craft of *bidri-ware* (below), creates a six-runged ladder.

embossed sheet vinyl, a hard-surfaced flooring that changes its face to suit the company it keeps. Parquet, marble, terrazzo, brick, ceramic tile and flagstone are but a few of the materials that vinyl can simulate. Vinyl first came to the fore with the checkerboard, black-and-white-tile floor, a simulated version of the classic marble pattern, that rapidly became a decorating cliché.

Nothing is as versatile as vinyl. Wood-grain vinyl or tiles in the rambling outline of flagstones or a herringbone brick pattern can be unrolled to suit the surroundings. Laminates include the genuine materials – wood veneers, cane, pebbles, mother of pearl – encased in clear vinyl to allow the original texture to be seen beneath a hard, sleek protective surface.

Cork tiles, made from cork granules and a binding agent, compressed and then baked, were the common 1970s floor for the then young modern. Now these tiles are more often replaced with linoleum, a good, natural material made from ground cork, wood, flour, linseed oil and resins on a jute or hessian backing.

2 Rubber flooring laid in sheets, and

4 Trenches cast in the polished concrete floor were originally used to carry power lines in this old electricity generation plant. When converting it into a home, architect Gary Cunningham used the trenches to carry the domestic electricity cables, covered with triple-laminate armoured glass to – figuratively – shocking effect. The table on castors reinforces that tramline imagery.

5 This metal landing, looking not unlike a diver's platform on top of an oil rig, has narrow cable grips conjuring all the thrills of the trapeze artist's ascent. At rooftop level, steel walkways give the security of additional support underfoot.

ribbed or studded, was a high-tech favourite in the 1970s. Modern tiles of synthetic resins mixed with a vinyl binder are important pattern makers, often replicating the grand piazzas found in Italy, and sometimes producing a giddy *trompe-l'oeil* effect.

An exciting innovation in contemporary floor covering is the wall-to-wall patterned carpet revitalized by the German company Vorwerk in collections commissioned from artists, architects and fashion designers from around the world. Using conventional broadloom mass-production machines, and a new ICI thread known as Timbrelle, any shading of colour can be controlled by

6 & 7 Jan Kaplicky of Future Systems used aluminium sheet on chipboard panels for a false floor laid above the existing 19th-century floorboards in this city apartment (see detail above).

The view through the space-shuttle doorframe, rendered in wide steel, shows the effect of the burnished floor and its black walkways, leading to a Rietveld chair beyond. Underneath this platform floor, gas, electricity and water pipes are concealed. Because the floor is metal, the electricity supply has to be earthed on it for safety.

8 Like a stage set from Hertzog's film "Fitzcarraldo", this weird jungle home in Mexico, by Sergio Puente and Ada Dewes, makes a totemistic room arrangement. Rough-adzed tree-trunk architraves against the regular grid pattern of modern window panes are replicated in the floor, with reinforced opaque glass blocks set into colourless concrete.

9 The sloping eaves, with a huge skylight to bring necessary light into the interior, make it impracticable to walk into this attic space, so the architects Munkenbeck & Marshall caused the floor to fall away to allow the light to find its way below. A strategically placed steel walkway, ringed with tubular-steel railings, creates a strut wide enough to accommodate the television.

43

1 Architect David Wild has laid pewtery grey-blue, rubber-studded sheet flooring here in his own house. Being hard-wearing and practical, it provides a dramatic, workmanlike home office floor that is flexible enough to withstand things toppling over onto it.

2 Subtle smudge colours of the Dutch 17th-century master class are accurately used in sheet vinyl by Tarkett, whose sunburst "Eminent" is also available in borders, friezes and decorative edgings for designing grand floors in a contemporary material.

3, 4 & 5 As more architects discover, linoleum is more than just a hard-wearing floor covering – it is an extremely versatile material that can be

cut to produce unique designs. Krommenie "Marmoleum" sheet linoleum from Forbo Nairn can be hot-welded to give a seam-free surface.

computer to produce a result that accurately reflects an original work of art. The low ceiling, the bugbear of contemporary apartments, is offset by these striking designs, which direct the eye firmly down, rather than up. Only a seriously wealthy collector can afford a Hockney these days, but with this new carpet technology you can afford to trample one underfoot.

More conventional contemporary interiors are turning to the anonymous naturals, such as rush matting, coconut and coir or sisal, backed with latex for easy laying. Those softer, golden colours of sea-grass, jute or fibre matting are a splendid background to a collection of rugs, each one a work of art in itself. The new mobility of today's society makes these rugs a realistic investment, since monied nomads can roll them up and take them away when they move

6, 7 & 8 "Metro" synthetic rubber tiles from Gerflor are available in a choice of stud relief patterns and thicknesses – 2.5 mm thick in round, square and pavé, and 3.5 mm thick in either round or square. A wide range of primary and neutral colours are available to suit most decorative schemes.

9 Forbo Nairn's "Diamond 1036" cushion-vinyl material, in subtle shades of lilac and grey, is a stylish as well as a practical option for kitchen flooring.

10 In his home, architect Andreas Weber has rubber flooring, in discreet cream for his dining-room, which he then accentuates by an exaggerated sense of scale – the low radiator, an oversized console table, the furniture in general. But throughout, the material is an anonymous, sound-proofed background.

12 Linoleum provides the base for dramatic designs by Forbo Nairn. The material is made from linseed oil, resin from pine trees, wood from deciduous trees and cork, mixed with fillers such as clay and chalk, calendered onto a hessian back.

13, 14 & 15 "Prism," smooth-surfaced rubber tiles from Gerflor, have an inlaid chip decoration and are tough enough for use in high traffic areas.

16 Rubber floor tiles, like these made by RIAB, can be a "green" product if they are made from recycled tyres.

11 Subtle gradations of natural brown and grey shades are combined in "Rocky" – a domestic vinyl flooring from Tarkett's "Manhattan" range – in order to impart an appropriate impression of weight and solidity, as well as an all-important sense of comfort and warmth to a room.

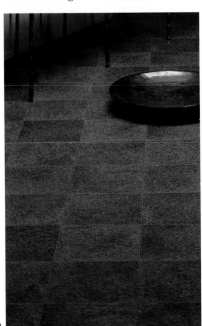

home, in much the same way as people have always done, ever since pre-historic times.

In rooms where the architecture is bland and the furniture simple, a richly patterned rug, in relief, brings the decoration down to earth to focus interest and attention on the floor and to define a scattered furniture grouping. A simple, striped rug can visually make a room appear to be much wider or longer than it actually is; a circular rug, in addition to determining the configuration of, perhaps, a seating or dining group, also gives tables and chairs a more compelling background. The flamboyance of the colours and the scale of the pattern are deliberately calculated to initiate a dramatic and vibrant scheme in a neutral room, in much the same way as the addition of an enormous abstract painting does.

17 A high-quality vinyl flooring from Amtico, whose simulations of genuine materials combine natural beauty with the practicality of a man-made product.

45

1 Ege Art Line's "20th Century Masters Collection" (see **3**) includes "Woman/Femme 1923" by René Magritte.

2 "Peau d'ours" rug by Pucci de Rossi for Neotu is made of hand-tufted wool, outlining the undulating shape of a polar bear. Ironically, black studs on big slabs suggest hard flooring, an illusion sustained all in wool.

3 Ege Art Line produce the "20th Century Masters Collection"– 48 pure wool rugs to designs by world-famous artists. This example is "Composition-1952" by Gunnar Aagaard Andersen.

4 This design, "Blue Eye," is by Gianni Veneziano of the Oxido group. It was made for the Italian group, Sisal Collezioni.

5 Christine van der Hurd's memorable collection of elegant floor coverings is reminiscent of the luxuriant 1920s and 30s. This design is called "Earth".

6 "Rustic Ruins Number 2" is by Liz Kitching, whose designs are painted on canvas floorcloths, worked into tufted wool rugs or made into hooked rugs, which are created entirely of recycled textiles.

7 A tendency to break up smooth surfaces and regular lines is evident in all areas of design. Cartoonist turned interior designer Javier Mariscal created for Mariscal this artwork of the slinky Pink-Panther-like creature called "Leon".

8 Pascal Mourgue's "Espace du Temps", for Toulemonde Bouchart, refers to the origin of the species, he claims. His technique, even here in wool, reflects his training at the *Ecole des Arts Decoratifs*, and wood-carving skills at the *Ecole Boulle*.

9 "Yuyuka" by Sergio Calatroni for Sisal has a biscuit-coloured ground with cabalistic signs, blue arrows and a red and green border.

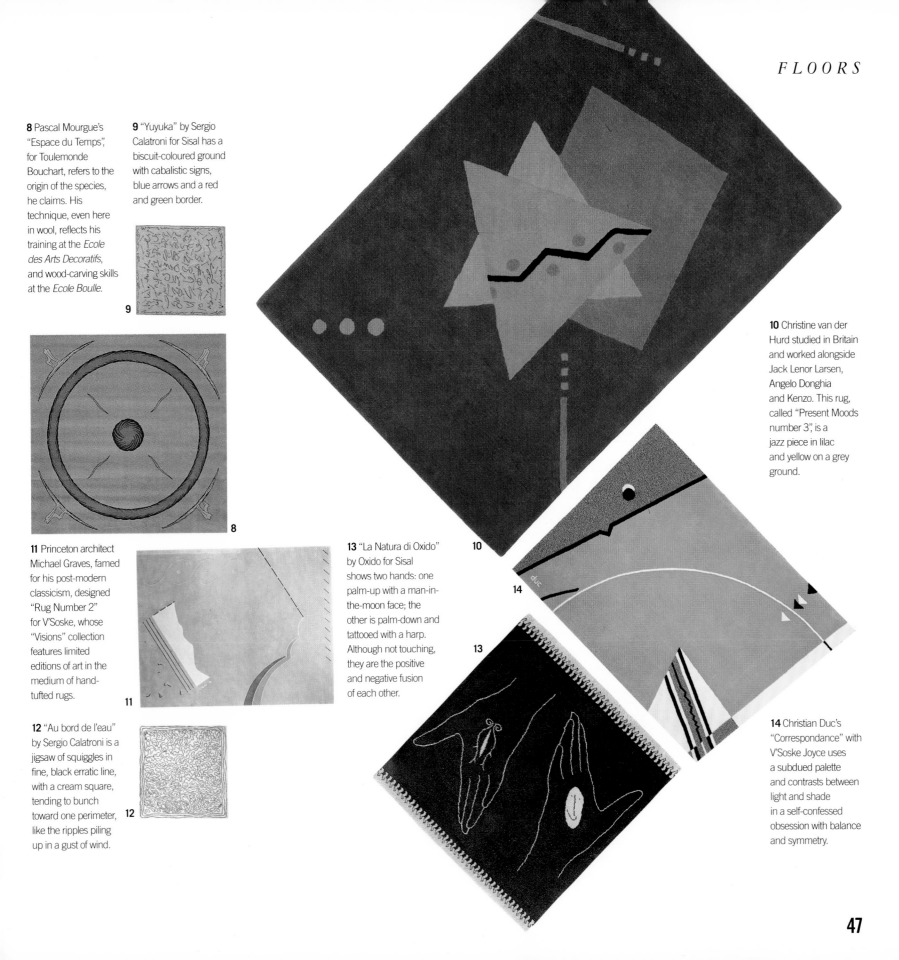

10 Christine van der Hurd studied in Britain and worked alongside Jack Lenor Larsen, Angelo Donghia and Kenzo. This rug, called "Present Moods number 3", is a jazz piece in lilac and yellow on a grey ground.

11 Princeton architect Michael Graves, famed for his post-modern classicism, designed "Rug Number 2" for V'Soske, whose "Visions" collection features limited editions of art in the medium of hand-tufted rugs.

12 "Au bord de l'eau" by Sergio Calatroni is a jigsaw of squiggles in fine, black erratic line, with a cream square, tending to bunch toward one perimeter, like the ripples piling up in a gust of wind.

13 "La Natura di Oxido" by Oxido for Sisal shows two hands: one palm-up with a man-in-the-moon face; the other is palm-down and tattooed with a harp. Although not touching, they are the positive and negative fusion of each other.

14 Christian Duc's "Correspondance" with V'Soske Joyce uses a subdued palette and contrasts between light and shade in a self-confessed obsession with balance and symmetry.

FLOORS

"Dialog 1", "Dialog 2" and "Classic" are collections of wall-to-wall carpets by Vorwerk. Using the designs of artists, architects and fashion designers, these mass-produced, affordable acrylic broadloom carpets closely resemble the originals in line, colour and shading.

1 Concurrent with their "Dialog" collection, Vorwerk also produce masterpieces in their "Classic" collection, like this carpet from Josef Hoffmann, a member of the avant-garde Vienna Secession dating from 1898 to 1903.

2 Pop artist Roy Lichtenstein demanded absolute pure white as a background, an impossibility in carpet manufacture. Vorwerk managed to overcome the problem in their reproduction of his small-scale squared design in which the black and white diagonally striped squares break the bounds of their form.

3 Artist Gerhard Richter uses both brush and palette knife to apply glowing colour. This effect is reproduced in his design for Vorwerk, which consists of squares in six different colours, a reminder of the artist's 1970s experimentation with paint manufacturers' colour cards. The pattern repeat consists of 5.5 x 7.5 inches (14 x 19 cm), within an overall repeat size of 39 x 36 inches (100 x 92 cm), which totals 255 squares, with the result that even in the repeat sequence the visual impression is one of an irregular and a random colour field.

4 Zaha Hadid is an architect whose dizzying viewpoint of urban planning – and building – can be seen in this blueprint of a design for a hillside recreational club above Hong Kong's harbour.

5 Architect Richard Meier's fascination with geometry – his buildings are based on a clearly defined stuctural grid – is immediately obvious in the blue-printed façades and street plans he created as a carpet pattern for Vorwerk.

6 Painter David Hockney transfers his constant variations on a paintbrush line to his carpet design, with brushstrokes that appear almost to be randomly placed in optimistic colours. Vorwerk have managed to transfer this sense of the rapid application of small spots of colour to their carpeting reproduction of Hockney's work.

7

7 The dodecahedron, which O. M. Ungers uses as the base for his carpet design, makes the polyhedron within appear to shift from being closer to the viewer, to farther away. As a result, this puzzling block pattern literally shifts perspective. Like Italian Renaissance flooring designs, *trompe l'oeil* banding alternates dark and light to give an unsettling, visual effect.

9

8 Architect Arata Isozaki's carpet design was inspired by Japanese period kimono dye patterns, which break down geometric, cosmic and floral elements into dots for an interwoven, pointillist effect.

9 This design is by architect Jean Nouvel, whose Institut du Monde Arab in Paris responds to the moving sun as light-sensitive lenses on the façade open and close in the manner of camera shutters.

This preoccupation with light and shade is shown here in his dazzling carpet for Vorwerk.

8

8 Ruckstuhl believe in giving their floorings a clear identity in terms of both colour and tone, yet never allowing them to domi-nate other furnishings. They claim that this "diagonal/transverse" weave in natural coir and sisal fibre is a perfect background.

6 & 7 Crucial Trading's "Natural Seagrass" floor covering, available in 13- and 6.5-feet (4- and 2-m) latex-backed widths, has a thread of bold colour interwoven with the plaited, natural seagrass.

1, 2 & 3 Hard-wearing and anti-static sisal, coir and seagrass from Saraband are all available with latex backing, in 13-feet (4-m) widths to be close-fitted like traditional carpeting. Or they can be supplied as a loose-laid mat or runner to virtually any size. Herringbone (above), bouclé (middle) and standard (below) weaves are available.

4 All Japanese houses are built around the standard-sized tatami mats, which blend so well with modern design. The Japanese pioneered modular building, since all timber sizes follow the mat-sizing procedure.
5 Bosanquet Ives popular herringbone jute, 36 inches (91 cm) wide, is joined by jute in basket weaves, also 36 inches (91 cm) wide, either in all-natural or crosswoven with scarlet-, emerald- or Baltic-blue threads.

9 As well as carpets in coir and sisal plant fibre, such as the "Pianelle" design shown here, Ruckstuhl make flooring in pure new wool, goats' hair and natural fibre wools. Styles range from wall-to-wall installations to edge-bound area rugs, throw rugs and even carpet tiles.
10 Crucial Trading's "Candy Stripe" sisal collection combines tonal colours and contrasts them with two-colour weaves on the diagonal.

11 Loose-laid coir and sisal tiles from Crucial Trading measure nearly 20 inches (50 cm) square. Produced in bleached or natural finishes, they are hard-wearing and ideal in heavy traffic areas, with effective thermal, acoustical and anti-static properties.

Doors

The door is both the first thing a visitor sees on entering your home and the last thing on leaving. We all have doors—front and back and internally for the division of space. Yet most of us seem to take no notice of them, choosing to live with the doors supplied in modern houses today. There they stand, a standard 6 feet 6 inches by 2 feet 8 inches (198 cm by 81 cm), either panelled or plain and usually equipped with a door handle or pull. This is why most homes, even those that are imaginatively decorated inside, look boringly the same from the outside.

However, there are many good, interesting alternatives to experiment with, all of which are fully functional and meet the requirements of excluding draughts, sound and light, as well as offering necessary security.

Making an entrance that is dramatically different yet in keeping with the house's style, character and architecture can be as simple as changing the door proportions. These were laid down in the 18th century when the rules dictated that the door height should be twice, or a little more than twice, its width. More varied in their ratio of dimensions, contemporary doors can significantly alter the apparent height of rooms by slimming down or stretching further the door itself. Architects Trevor Horne and John Pawson both use this visual trick to increase the appearance of height in low-ceilinged rooms. They use custom-built doors that are taller than normal and that operate on pivot hinges within the frames in order

Previous page From architectural practice GMW, triangular glazed insets set into double doors highlight the position of the door handles and provide a tantalizing glimpse into the space beyond.

1

2

1 & 2 In this apartment restoration, Studio Epton's fastidious attention to detail frames each door with ornamental handles or pulls, either in pairs or singles, which reduce the bulk and display a geo- metric rearrangement of everyday, domestic functionalism.
3 One of the greatest views in California is here framed by a pair of folding doors at the Villa Zapu by the former team of Powell-Tuck, Connor and Orefelt.

3

4 Irregular but geo-
metrically configured
black-timbered frames
outline glass doors.
Three stone steps mark
the ascent into this
house by architect
Sergio Puente. Inside,
an evenly paced
wooden staircase set
below a horizontal
skylight is on view in
this entrance.

4

5

6

5 Corrugated acrylics
in four folding panels
casually yet effectively
screen an office with
interiors designed
by Stefano de Martino.
Slimline hinges
clench the sinuous
panels together.
6 Architect
Jan Kaplicky's space-
capsule approach to an
apartment conversion,
set within a 19th-
century townhouse,
has a normal-sized
door covered in steel-
mesh and set in
a widened, reinforced
steel frame.

53

DOORS

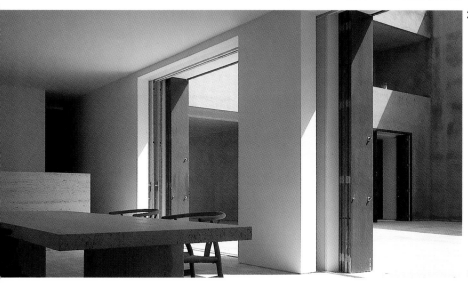

1 & 2 For a custom-built Majorcan villa the former architectural partnership of Claudio Silvestrin and John Pawson used a pair of monumental folding doors on the inside, mirrored in mass and volume by the exterior set which lead out onto a sunken tennis court.

3 With the marketplace in the US driven by demand for period architectural styles, the modernists are left to fend for themselves, says architect Mark Marcinik, whose new company created these bi- or tri-folding doors in hardwood veneered plywood with an aluminium trim.

4 A pair of beech doors, made from American hardwood and set in a monumental architrave, are lightened with a checkerboard grid of glass panes.

to avoid revealing unsightly hardware. As large houses are carved up into smaller apartments, which are then adapted to contemporary living, unbroken wall space is what every architect dreams of. This explains architects' common obsession with eliminating unnecessary entrances. Their aim is to reduce the impact of those entrances that remain with discreet doors. Sometimes, they alter proportions by widening the gap and lowering the height. In such a case architect Pierre d'Avoine always frames the broader view glimpsed through the space with

5 This old wooden Japanese inn was reassembled on a small suburban plot. Inside, the room dimensions are based on the sizes of four, six or eight tatami mats. Shoji screens and mud walls are new, built to open on only two sides, instead of the traditional four.

6 Lynn Davis designed this beech door with two squares on the top corners, which replicate the rosewood inlaid cube and narrow arrow slit.

7 These doors by Rehabitec Y Diseno are made of beech with inset glass keyhole-shaped windows acid-etched, and framed in stainless steel. Architects normally remove doors to free space, but this corridor effect has an interesting theatrical impact.

8 A stylish entrance door to an apartment in American white oak veneer shows off the ash inlay used within the grooved and imposingly wide frame. The US has huge hardwood resources, with some 6 million soft- and hardwood trees planted daily.

11 Armstrong Associates give a substantial entrance a light treatment by splitting two panels in the wooden door with a glass border, through which the giant-sized floor-to-ceiling tubular-steel grips used on either side can be clearly seen.

7

8

dark-wood mahogany or oak posts either side to support the architrave. The way in which doors fasten is another troubling issue, since the plain, modern doors of today, uncluttered with panelling or finger plates, key rings or any extravagant and unnecessary door furniture, must silently and unobtrusively pivot or slide in their frames. Often the door frame is made of wood, fireproofed and burglar-proofed since it is by breaking the door jamb that most forced entries are effected. Entablatures with pilasters and Venetian heads flanking the door in the classical manner – a style still enforced with grandeur by neoclassicists – are no substitute for the security offered by a strong frame and a well-hung door. In terms of security, front doors in Italy are armour-plated with large, mirrored, bullet-proof glass that allows light into the home while offering occupants a clear view outside. A polyester finish disguises their invulnerability behind care-free colour.

Sliding-panel double internal doors, which pull back on either side of an opening to flank it like Japanese shoji

9

9 Trompe-l'oeil lattice detailing created by skillfully inlaid woods brings a classical façade and an impression of three-dimensionality to a flat wooden door. John Outram is a Post-Modern architect whose work employs the decorative flourishes of the 18th-century cabinet-maker to create a refreshing alternative to period-style mouldings.

10 Wooden doors do not have to be straight-edged, as this curved jigbit in American oak proves. Its organically shaped handles serve to emphasize that timbered fluidity.

10

11

screens, are a popular alternative to conventional doors. They depend, however, on unbroken wall space at the sides to accommodate the doors as they slide across.

Without panelling and decoration, doors in modern homes are usually hot-spray-painted to give a continuous, smooth surface, either matte or gloss. Mass-produced modern doors are lacquered or made of fruit woods burnished to bring out the patina of the material. Exciting alternatives include doors designed by De Pas, D'Urbino and Lomazzi which are both concave and convex – a sinuous curve like a bow with polyurethane-foam injections

1 "Radar" by Tre P is a reversible door, made from lacquered wood. Tre P's modern, linear design can be fixed to open either left or right. Patented hinges are well camouflaged.

2 Three little purple glass panels set into the circular glassed stairwell echo the purple front to this door, with its semi-circular grips that are lit for night time.
4 Specially curved glass doors in John Young's riverside home lead to the laundry and bathroom. They are flanked by steel lift doors.

3 Dierre's "AT 4" door pleasantly conceals the fact that it is armour-plated, with a tongue-and-grooved panelling in electrically galvanized, reinforced double-steel plate.

It is painted white and set in a black frame with a special, safe-type lock concealed behind high-density polystyrene to give perfect heat and sound insulation.

5 Medieval castles have portcullised entrances reached by a moated fort. This house with red-brick ramparts has a glass-block grid that replicates the ancient portcullis above a human-sized door with a spyhole.

6 This front door within an inner courtyard is convex, with a red-painted frame. It is surrounded by clapboard panelling that is asymmetrically arranged with narrow boards on one side and wider ones on the other. Designed by architect Eric Owen Moss, this external door opens inward and its red frame effectively delineates the entrance.

7 Another view of the unusually shaped design by architect Eric Owen Moss, shown in picture **6**.

8 The Lualdi door, "Super", by Luigi Caccia Dominioni, is the world's first polyester lacquered door, with a horizontal, slimline steel grip emphasized by the scarlet background.

sandwiched between. They feature four dots at eye level, inside which a night light is inserted to make it easy for people to find their way at night.

Also available are silent sliding doors in red lacquer that fold flat like the wings of a butterfly against the wall, leaving only the black lacquer door frame around the entrance. These take up very little room and they are reversible so that they can be hung to the left or right.

Sometimes a small, overall pattern proliferates, like the Braille punch-card pattern in the "Egizia" collection designed by Toso and Massaria, the discreet pattern of which won't over-power the interior. Custom effects are sometimes used – architect Alessandro Mendini stencilled a leaf pattern in shades of green on exterior doors of an Italian lakeside villa to bring the garden

10 Tre P's "Rever" door, designed by architect Cini Boeri with Laura Griziotti and Guido Nardi, is made of leaf timber with a hollow core. Its design allows the opening direction to be decided at the last moment.

9 The angularity of this pair of doors, set within a corner, is offset by the triangular sky panel above. Architect Lynn Davis's design replicates the light that falls between these two doors, exaggerated by the red triangular door handles.

2 Too often, garage doors bear no resemblance to the house they adjoin. Here, an inner, open courtyard with glazed walls is shielded from sunlight by louvred, horizontal blinds from Faber, that display a distinct relationship to the ridged aluminium garage doors to the right. The design is by architect Robin Spence.

1 A breakfast bar in tubular steel is flanked by a pair of French doors that open outward onto a balcony. Large, vertical tubular-steel handles on the outside and inside mirror each other. Brick, steel and glass are appropriate in this contemporary make-over of a riverside warehouse, designed by architect John Young.

3 Front doors from the street to this house have two-storey height glass doors inserted between floors with a semi-circular steel-mesh balcony girded with railings. The doors, in fact, are four double doors, the divisions between them hidden by the balcony. Ten panes of glass on each door form a lattice. The handles operating on the nearside of the doors are lockable from the inside or out.

4 This multi-fold door from Wing Industries flattens against the wall like a screen when drawn back, yet provides privacy when pulled across the entrance without blocking the light.

closer to the structure of the house. In older houses it was often necessary to insert fanlights above the door, leaded or in stained glass, to allow light to filter in, but the nature of modern interiors obviate this necessity. Stained-glass door panels designed by the American architect Frank Lloyd Wright at the turn of the 20th century, in the style he termed "Usonian" (US-onian), have now been put into mass produc-tion. At a time when the Arts and Crafts glassmakers in Europe were producing the sinuous lilies and vines of the Art Nouveau period, Wright's stained-glass

5 The Simpson 15-lite bevelled French door in the "Mastermark" series has thermal panes.

7 & 8 Three glass screens, one in the middle hinged so that it opens into the dining room, hide the working kitchen from the dining area very effectively, without blocking the light or separating these two related rooms. The house is by Gianfranco Cavaglia.

door panels show an angularity and geometric formalism – as do his buildings. In rectilinear designs and primary colours, his doors mirror the type of home he pioneered: suburban houses that spread outward, instead of upward like the terraced houses of a cramped Europe. Wright used concrete breeze-block latticed screens to form that vital link between inside and outside.

6 Inserting light panels in doors is the nearest the modern architect comes to pattern-making. In contemporary doors there are the blocks of opaque glass arranged like Josef Hoffman's stacking

9 To create his own London home, architect Sir Richard Rogers gutted and combined two 19th-century terraced houses and removed most of the doors to create a soaring space that is full of light. To hold the light that streams in through 16 windows, the opaque glass door, with its simple vertical, tubular-steel grip, creates a partition without making the doorway into a set piece.

6 Customized, glass floor-to-ceiling French doors have been laser cut to a wavy template.

1 In a warm climate the door doesn't have to insulate the home. This tubular-steel door by Franklin D. Israel is appropriately open to the elements, yet still secure with a grille reaching top to bottom.

grids, two-thirds of the way up the door—aesthetic as well as illuminating. Now that brass hardware in period styles is clumsily irrelevant to door fastening, the modern door handle has been the subject for architects and designers to sculpt new shapes and banish chrome anonymity. The newest handles incorporate light-sensitive materials that glow softly in the dark. To humanize technology it is necessary to have a high-touch, not a high-tech approach. Organic, root-like door hardware by the Spanish architect Antonio Gaudí is still produced today. The designs go back to 1904 — proof indeed that door design can become a classic and play its part in the modern home. Generally, casement and panel doors have fallen from their pedestalled architrave, since their broken fussiness detracts from the simple entrance

2 This perforated stainless steel entry door, at mid-level in a tri-plex penthouse in New York by architect Steven Forman, swings open from the vestibule at the touch of a finger. Made by Treitel Gratz Inc,

the vertical light troughs that run the length of this long, narrow house are made of opaque glass brick and block from PPG Pittsburgh Corningware.

3 In this former factory, architect Ben Kelly uses a steel front door with a contemporary fanlight above it. Unusually, the steel door is set within a wooden frame – a reversal of traditional roles. The steel is

acid-etched to give a mottled, rubbed patina. This play of textures is picked up in the horsehair matting and small block parquet on the floor, set against a rough-adzed, dark-stained wooden wall.

favoured in the contemporary home. The louvred door, behind which most storage took place in the bedroom and bathroom, has also fallen from favour. Bi-fold doors, pivoted at the side and centrally hung on accordion tracks, are now more popular. The newest mechanisms for wooden folding doors are ones that concertina across large spans, dividing dining from living spaces, for example, or dressing from study areas, when necessary. These doors are as versatile as a screen, while practically eliminating draughts and noise, and they take up less space than an ordinary door. Since they are for interior use, these doors are usually made from high-density particle board faced with a range of wood veneers or water-resistant vinyl.

An insecure door lets in draughts, noise and, worst of all, intruders. Magnetic fasteners on interior doors preclude draughts and noise and, for the front and back doors, there are secure door-jamb and mortice-type locks (one set into the full thickness of the door), or the slam-action door lock with a strong, deadlocking bolt.

Fitting a sturdy door chain and viewer, with front bolts for outward-opening doors, gives added protection. And on outward-opening doors where the hinges are exposed, there is the hinge bolt that engages every time you close the door. Two bolts fitted in each door within a few inches of the hinges help to form solid protection between the door and frame.

4

5

6

4 For a city apartment, architect Eva Jiricna uses steel doors that are reminiscent of submarine hatches, with a glass peep-hole at eye level, and silvered handles.

5 Irish-born designer Clodagh, working in the United States, favours patina finishes, such as unpainted plaster. This blue patina door in painted steel, by David Johnson for Clodagh Design International, has a Harrison door handle and copper lock. Clodagh's interior designs rely upon the good looks of the basic materials of the construction industry – glass, plaster, concrete and steel.

6 Stainless steel lift doors provide an interesting surface alongside a steel security door that has a surveillance camera and entry door formula installed by Castle Security Services.

DOORS

1 Unlike most metallic fittings, Hewi's nylon-covered steel handles and grips do not become uncomfortably cold to the touch during the winter.

2 "Sarissa" brass handles, from Valli and Colombo's "Casual" collection of decorative door handles and fittings, are available in polished brass, chrome, white, black and opaque matte-black finishes.

5 A lever handle from Ambrose Mortez's "Baia" series for Mandelli. The special shock-resistant "Fluxcoat" finish enhances the brightness of the brass.

6 Philip Hearsey's scarlet lacquered internal doors are crowned with a pair of heavy-duty, front door ring pulls, their brass finish patinated with ammonia fumes.

3 Designed by Stephen George, these polished "Best of Brass" handles can either be bolted directly to the chosen door, or else affixed with a round or rectangular backplate.

4 Angelo Becchetti handles, knobs, hinges, door pulls and knockers are made of polished, lacquered brass. The "Erika" handle was designed by their in-house BAL studio.

7 FSB commission door handles from famous designers. Model "1184", by Franco Berg, accords with the company's belief that "one can only grasp a thing of substance".

8 Looking like a patch of blue sky, the square-plated "Modric" unit from Allgood incorporates a horizontal lever handle designed to sit flush like a simple door pull.

9 A choice of brass, chrome and polished black metal finishes is available for these door pulls designed by Josep Llusca and produced by the Sellex foundry in Spain.

10 Neo-baroque door knobs and handles designed by Gerard Dalmon and gilded or bronze-patinated by avant-garde company, Neotu.

11 & 12 "Vienna" 1 and 3 are from a collection of solid brass door fittings, finished in polished brass or matte black. They have been designed ergonomically for easy handling, by Ivo Pelligri for RDA.

13 Exact reproductions, both in form and in hand-polished solid brass, of eight original designs from the turn of the century by the great architect Antonio Gaudí, include this unusual vertebraic door handle, engraved with his signature, by Bd Ediciones de Diseno.

14 Christian Cirici used twirls of congoy or coral wood clasped in polished or chromed brass for the bracelet-like pull handle from the graceful "Herrajes Bd" range he designed for Bd Ediciones de Diseno – a series which also includes a door knob, a catch for a sliding door and a furniture knob.

15 Briarwood handle with brass rosette and escutcheon from the "Otto F" series by Gianfranco Frattini for Fusital.

16 "Bridge" handle, by Guiseppe Raimondi for Eurobrass.

17 Frascio's brass "Piramide" handles, by Paolo Nava, are made impervious to corrosion.

18 "Cormorano" brass fittings from Valli and Colombo's "Classic" collection.

19 "Fenix", a sinuously shaped, solid brass handle designed by Guiseppe Raimondi for Eurobrass's "Design Collection" of door furniture.

DOORS

1 This smooth operator, a satin-finish, stainless steel bolt designed by Alan Tye for Allgood's "Modric" series, is suitably reinforced to slot into a steel door frame, if required for reasons of security.

2 Hewi's colourful "625" sprung-nylon doorstop offers a smooth, silent action and minimizes the risk of accidents.

3 Design "1138" from Dieter Rams' "rgs" range for FSB. The combination of grey aluminium and black plastic underlines his philosophy that simplicity surpasses complexity.
4 Design "1102", by architect Alessandro Mendini for FSB, is a re-design of the lever handle famous Bauhaus designer Walter Gropius created for the Fagus Works in the 1920s.
5 Designed by Alan Tye for Allgood's "Modric" series of door furniture, the "Unilite" is made of a luminous PVC that glows in the dark and is re-charged by either natural or artificial light. It is ideal for bathrooms.

6 A solid-looking, suitably angular chrome lever handle complements the thick custom-made glass and black door frame in David Wild's house.

7 The human hand meets mechanical component in the mellifluous fluidity of Mario Botta's door handle design "1104" for FSB.

8 & 9 FSB lever "1144" and knob "2374" are "unassuming and usable products" by Jasper Morrison.

10 James Hong's aluminium plate door-pull for CDI is designed to fit any sliding glass door.

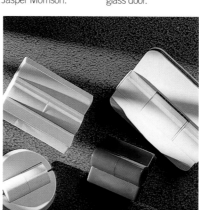

14 Hewi conceal their colourful fixings with nylon caps and covers. One intention behind this is that even when a door is open its hinges will still look neat – which is not always the case with painted hinges.

11 Fire-door hinges need to be made of reinforced steel and have strong fastening bolts, like the stainless steel model designed by Alan Tye for the "Modric" range and manufactured by Allgood, the architectural hardware specialists.

12 A doorstop designed by Knud Holscher for Carl F. Petersen's stainless steel and polished brass "d-line" range.

13 The "M" lever handle designed by Knud Holscher for Carl F. Petersen's "d-line" range features an anti-vandal/thief fixing plate.

15 The Stuttgart Design Centre awarded a prize to the stainless steel "WSD 88" by Walter Schnepel for Tecnolumen, who produce original Bauhaus designs as well as fittings by today's designers.

Windows

G lass is the most innovative building material of the 20th century. Architects are constantly exploring new ways of using this one medium that is intrinsic to both the interior and exterior of the building. Windows open the home to light and air; they are its eyes and lungs. But as they rapidly transform into its skin, their role is changing from being simply windows to being the walls themselves. These glass façades have brought their own problems, however, as inhabitants seek to muffle them with drapes to give privacy as well as protection from sunlight.

As the century draws to a close there are signs of a revolutionary new development in windows for contemporary housing. Technological developments within the glass-making industry have produced a type of glass that allows those on the inside to see out but presents an opaque surface to those trying to look in. This glass is also photosensitive, darkening as the light intensifies and lightening once more at dawn when light levels are low. The French architect

1 Wood technology prevails in this Gwathmey Siegel house, which has a formal grid of different shaped windows creating a pleasing pattern while bathing the interior with light.

1

2

3

Previous page
Bigger panes of glass, stronger sealing materials and fittings capable of invisibly holding great spans of glass have changed the shape of modern windows. They open outward, pivot inward, flap up, batten down and slide. The lines of this window's black metal frames are echoed in the slats of the Venetian blinds hanging inside. The design is by David Wild.
2 & 3 The former partnership of Claudio Silvestrin and John Pawson designed these windows. Their placement at the end of a long, tall corridor creates an unusual effect – the rectangular strips of glass catch the sun as it tracks across the sky during the day, casting a moving pattern of light and shade on the concrete floor below.

4

4 An entire wall of glass, braced with a metal gantry, has been built into architect John Young's riverside penthouse apartment. The effect is spectacular while, at the same time, demonstrating the remarkable industrial platecoil heater discs placed near the windowed wall for the best circulation of warmed air. Every third window on the second level can be opened, and three windows at the far wall act as a door onto the balcony.

5

5 In this view of John Young's riverside apartment, four floors above street level, his bathroom tower protrudes from the roofline. Its glass-brick walls double up as its windows. The bathroom tower, made of a braced-steel frame infilled with translucent glass blocks, has a clear glass roof.

1 Even the tubular-steel gate has been designed by architect David Wild to frame this line-up of windows, an arrangement of clear-glass blocks stacked to form a horizontal pattern above an amber slab of recessed wall. On the ground floor, visible from the street, frosted-glass cubes have been used, while the second floor features large panes of transparent glass screened by Venetian blinds.
2 Just a few doors away, another David Wild design has produced windows that pivot open, like the wings of a butterfly.

Jean Nouvel dramatically illustrated, in his Arab Institute building in Paris, just how to clad a structure in this photo-sensitive material. The net effect is like a camera lens, which can admit more light as day dims toward night or less light when the sun is high and the light is at its brightest. Chameleon-like, these glass surfaces interact dynamically with the climate to meet the users' needs, as well as to make optimum use of energy.

The British architect Richard Rogers, who already describes as a dinosaur his technically advanced and controversial Lloyds Insurance building in London's financial district – the only landmark to be built this century in the capital – observes that constructions will "dematerialize" as architecture is no longer a question of mass and volume but of lightweight structures with superimposed transparent layers.

Such radical advances are all the more remarkable for their relative novelty. For centuries, loosely fixed waxed skins across gaps, or narrow apertures on crenellated walls, were the only way to bring daylight, and a view of the outside, into dwellings. The Iranians and then the Romans discovered how to

5 A grand piano, the Lloyd Loom wicker chairs, exotic flowers – every detail in this music room has been designed by architect Rick Mather to escape from the feeling of a conservatory addition. The giant incline of glass above, and the evenly paced windows below, create a space of light, yet cosy, intimacy.
6 Alexander Gorlin has employed three monumental sheets of glass, divided by square pillars, to allow light to stream into the building during the day and to flood out at night onto the swimming pool.

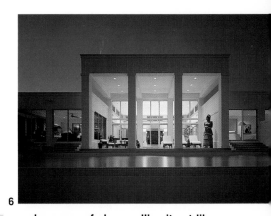

3 This house, designed by Lustig, has a perfect symmetry. The glass wall conforms to the geometry of the house, using square panes of glass that extend right up to the extravagant swooping eaves at roof level. The symmetry is confirmed by the room's focal point, a centrally located fireplace, as well as by two steel, cylindrical flues forming columns that are visible both inside and out.

4 The window range "Inoxfinestra" by Industrie Secco has been chosen by Spectrum for an office development consisting of a soaring stack of windows fixed in rectangular stainless steel frames.

7 Glass bricks bring light into David Chipperfield's inner city architectural practice, a building without the benefit of a view. For balance, there is a window panel of evenly paced square panes.

8 Two solid, immobile sheets of glass make up the corner of this living room in a David Chipperfield design. Selective openings reveal only that which the architect intended to frame, such as this courtyard.

make panes of glass, rolling it out like pastry when molten. But this product was cloudy, thick and shattered if made larger than a tiny pane. Nonetheless, the process lasted until the 19th century, with great banks of small panes in leaded surrounds creating the oriel window. A ubiquitous architectural feature for four centuries was the window seat, which provides a clue as to just how little daylight filtered through into the interior of houses. It was only in 1959 in England that molten glass was poured out of a furnace up to 11 feet (3.3 metres) wide and was capable of being shifted onto building sites. The evolution of glass became a revolution as monumental sheets of glass up to virtually any length were made which were strong enough to be supported on steel frames.

Planning strictures on buildings from earlier ages are designed to preserve the original façades, which accounts for the many diverse window shapes and sizes on the market. Conventional windows need restoration and dressing, according to the age of the structure. Older windows can be in the form of

WINDOWS

1 In the Trump Towers, New York, Gwathmey Siegel's use of wooden frames links a classical material to a modern building and helps it to stand out from the crowd in which metal and concrete predominate.

2 Modern windows such as these are usually found in aluminium casings, but Gwathmey Siegel amusingly converted the contemporary style by using wooden frames, varnished like rose-wood, in a wooden façade stained a metallic silvery grey.

1

3 The porthole, once banished to Art Deco architecture, enjoys a revival as a focal point in an avant-garde makeover in this house. Hinged to open irregularly, it can be secured from inside.

little outward-opening casements grouped in pairs; bays or bows; sash windows; arched windows; vertical dormer windows; or the porthole windows typical of the Art Deco period. Glass doors, known as French windows since their debut at Versailles in the 1680s, are casement windows carried to the floor where they open like doors, usually onto a patio or terrace of some description.

The clerestory window, the peaked, two-storey window in the A-frame house or post-modernist villa, and windows that turn the corner, such as those that the British architect David Chipperfield placed in the home of the fashion photographer Nick Knight, are some of the special casement windows that have made their appearance in the new architectural grid.

3 The loft or attic, which can be a third of

2

4

5

4 The south façade of the Villa Turque by Le Corbusier features this porthole, which, on the outside, is ringed with bricks and, on the inside, with an octagonal wooden template and lattice by Andrée Putman, the interior designer of the project.

5 Dovetailed corners in the cabinetmaker's fashion on a modern window fitting by Metall Kommerz are finely detailed with traditional brass hardware.

6 Metall Kommerz patented a window system called "Clima," which has perfect thermal insulation between the aluminium support and Canadian hemlock façade.

6

8 A stacked trio of wooden rectangular frames are set horizontally but open vertically, in this house by Gwathmey Siegel. A grid of glass blocks filters in additional light.

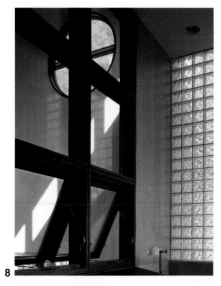

8

10 Pella Rolscreen frame windows and fixed skylight have been installed in an A-frame, with a ceiling fan suspended from the central crossbeam.

11

11 This sunroom features the vented Pella Rolscreen skylight and traditional french sliding door, which has double-glazed panels and insulated glass.

10

9

7 Architect Arata Isozaki has a reputation for designing some of the most beautiful modern art galleries. In this domestic setting, his windows are designed to bring maximum light and ventilation into the kitchen/dining area built beneath a pitched roof space.

9 The Pella Rolscreen entry door shows the circlehead fanlight in insulated glass – a fixed unit with glazed lintels, which brings a formal opening – and light – to a new residence.

12

12 Small, square, modern windows such as these are often eschewed by architects in favour of more grandiose schemes. But window manufacturers Metall Kommerz show how a plain,

white-painted window can be elaborated upon with a Georgian fanlight stencil. Replicating that image below the window as well as above makes an ironical, post-modernist joke of the scheme.

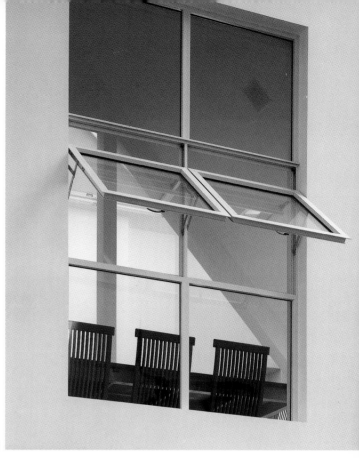

7

the total potential floor area inside a building, is being opened up to ease the squeeze on space. Roof windows providing light and ventilation in pitches angled as low as 15° have become popular. These windows open outward with an accessible handle on the sash and provide unobstructed views for anybody standing. On steeper inclines the windows open inward operated by a sash pull.

Whatever the style of building, there are frames to support the panes in metal, wood or plastic. Changes in buildings at both the functional and technological levels in the late 1960s and early 70s affected fittings such as windows, which traditionally had the merit of integrating craft skills with new innovations. Windows have always been manufactured, and often assembled, off-site. For centuries wooden window

13 Rolled-steel products for windows and doors from Industrie Secco combine the strength and economy of steel with polyester finishes, such as these frames from their "Seccolor" series.

13

1 A stunning window, designed by architect Peter Wilson, breaks up a glass wall with an acid-etched, delicate ribbed pattern on a background of frosted, opaque glass. This individual definition of a window brings plenty of light indoors while blocking a rather uninspiring mews courtyard view outside.

2 Stained-glass windows are heavy and this octagonal, domed rooflight had to be composed by Goddard and Gibbs in sections, supported by strong bars set in the roof.

3 Designer Philip Hearsey explores angles on squares with a sandblasted pattern of tiny squares on a vertical glass pane which is mimicked by the mosaic pattern of the stair carpet.

4 Goddard and Gibbs created this glass panel, spiralling in warm colours, to emphasize and enhance the coppery tone of the wood on the stairwell.

5 The thick cut glass in this window design by Jo Crepain distorts the light and the view outside. The advantage of this type of glass is that it forms the illusion of a translucent wall rather than of a definite window.

6 A modern interpretation of leaded glass by Jochem Poensgen uses float glass, mouth-blown opalescent, semi-opalescent and antique *danziger* glass.

6

7 An old electricity substation confronts its origins, and its conversion into a spacious residence, with this façade by architect Gary Cunningham. The supporting girders and the ceramic pylon contacts that clad the black-framed window emphasize and reinforce the electrical nature of the building, just as the owners intended.

4

7

frames dominated, but during the late 1960s there was a worldwide push for the mass production of windows to meet the need generated by the boom in housing, and other materials for frames, such as aluminium and plastic, were specified. Thus the first windows arrived from the standardized production line. Instead of windows being a craft product, external frames were transformed into just another building component. New materials – synthetic resin seals, treated aluminium sections, PVC (polyvinyl chloride) with alloys and steel, and all the impermeable plastics – joined forces on the assembly line to meet the new housing requirements. Frames today conform to a series of precise requirements imposed by building specifications. Windows must match standards for dimensional stability, fire safety, mechanical solidity, sound and heat insulation, lightness and long-term resistance to weather conditions. Energy saving is now being recognized as important, especially since windows are a major source of heat and energy loss. Resource conservation is also having an effect on windows. A campaign to halt the desecration of the Earth's tropical forests, without reafforestation and controlled felling, has made hardwoods such as teak an unpopular material. It is more likely, however, that hardwoods from temperate regions do come from managed plantations. Window dressing has always been an important interior consideration. According to the mood and manner of

8

8 Rectilinear music symbols were the inspiration behind this stained glass window by Patrick Ross-Smith. The lower panel was acid-etched from blue opal glass, the green panel is leaded.

9

9 Rashid Din of Din Associates designed this stylish assemblage of blue-smoked-glass and frosted-glass windows, which are emphasized by all being set in recessed moulded frames.

1

3

2

4

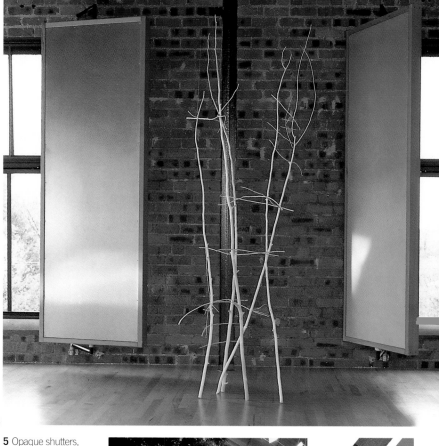

5

1 & 2 The popularity of plain roller blinds has receded in the wake of blinds with a ridged profile in Levolor's "Newport" range (**1**), and "Lyverscreen" solarscreens (**2**).

3 Faber's 16mm wide "Microlite" louvres fit into door panels and glazed room dividers with space-saving neatness.
4 Sunlight UK's "Light and Shade" shades in pleated polyester were made in 140 colours across five ranges. Opening and closing is with cordlock controls on overhead wands; there are also fully motorized systems.

the times, windows have been covered in every conceivable fashion, from the earliest draught-excluding tapestries to the lightest muslin sheers, or the more substantial alternatives such as wooden shutters. In the 21st century, contemporary details will render window dressing obsolete as the new generation of photosensitive glass does the job automatically. Then there will be something new under the sun.

Meanwhile, textile drapes are still under review in the contemporary interior. Architects are frequently asked to judge textile designs but they find draping a building in swathes of pattern, the way that a decorator does, something of a challenge. They can select patterned rugs for floors, but a piece of fabric is anathema to most modern architects.

In the contemporary interior, most rooms have a radiator panel placed under the window. But this cuts out the opportunity for long drops of fabric to cloak the window. As an alternative, the new wire mesh, paper, plastic laminate and fabric blinds offer an uninterrupted view when rolled up and some privacy

5 Opaque shutters, opening inward, veil the windows of this converted powerhouse, yet allow diffused light to enter when closed. While open, a complex hinge system lifts the shutters away from the windows.
6 The "Jalousien" range from Fönstret covers the walls and sloping, glazed skylight in this studio space by Anne Idstein. Louvred wooden slats, angled to any configuration, let in as much light as is required.

6

7

7 Timbershade Venetian blinds have Western red cedar 48mm or 25mm slats tinted in an extensive range of colours.

9

10

8

11

8 Opaque glazed bricks at garden level are topped by a grid of small panes of glass outlined in simple black frames in this custom-built house by David Wild.

9 Robin Spence used horizontal Venetian blinds from Faber throughout this house.

10 Vertical blinds are the obvious option for awkwardly shaped windows. Developments in tracking systems offer arched head, twin head, trapezoid and curved blinds, and these from the Louvre Blind Company show how the drawing mechanism works.

11 Franklin D. Israel's wide stretch of horizontal blinds leaves the eaves of this A-framed window wall free to allow unfiltered light to pour in, while offering privacy at street level.

and light when required. The techniques for designing these window coverings vary from the Austrian or festoon version, much-loved by decorators and generally considered vulgar by the design conscious, to the roller blind, which behaves exactly as its name suggests. Also included are the Roman type, which pulls up into accordion pleats on a cord; pinoleum and slatted wood blinds on a roller with a spring mechanism to set them at any level; and the architectural favourite, Venetian blinds, available with plastic, metal or wood slats.

On the outside, further details may be added. For example, the trellised metal grille that pulls over the window and locks in place is making something of a comeback in this security-conscious age, as is the exterior shutter.

1 Marimekko's 100 percent cotton prints make excellent Roman or roller blinds for contemporary homes, as the Finnish designed patterns are uncompromisingly modern. Designs shown here are "Sikerma" (bottom), "Ratamo" (middle), "Viikuna" (top).

2, 3, 4 & 5 Zimmer & Rohde produce a high-quality range of plain, woven textured and geometric fabrics that are particularly suitable for the windows of contemporary homes. Shown here are Thai silk (**2**), "Camelot" (**3**), silk canvas (**4**) and "Square Root" (**5**).

6, 7, 8, 9 & 10 Plain, textured and abstract patterned Thai silks from Jim Thompson (distributed by Mary Fox Linton) are used by contemporary designers like Charles Rutherfoord for window screens or banner-style curtains hung from simple steel, glass or metal poles. From the "Atmosphere" collection are "Luna" (**8** & **10**), "Pegasus" (**7**) and "Omega" (**9**).

11 Graphic stripes are the only pattern many contemporary designers allow. Sahco Hesslein produce a huge variety of stripes in a wide range of fibres – even the latest man-made mixtures – including "Zeno", a self-striped sateen; "Fontain," a multi-coloured sheer and "Ebro" corded velvet.

12 & 13 Jewel-coloured suede-like fabrics from Alicantara's "Master" range are suitable for heavy insulating curtains. Matching fabrics are available for covering walls and for upholstery.

14 Sahco Hesslein's crisply striped fabrics (see also picture **11** for variations) are available in a wide range of contemporary colourways.

Stairs

The movement afoot today in architectural interiors reveals itself in the structural simplicity of the staircases shown here, which resolve aspects of function in their sculptural form. As Nikolaus Pevsner put it so succinctly:

"In twentieth century architecture, the staircase assumes a new significance as the element in a building which is most expressive of spatial flow."

Skillful design solutions pace climbers, as well as acclimatize them to the lower ceilings and cramped quarters typical of buildings today, while deceiving viewers into believing that the space soars and that the ascent is simple. Since neither the Greeks nor the Romans were particularly interested in staircases in their villas, and the Medieval Age saw only some rudimentary ladders, it was not until the Regency period in England that the staircase sweeping upward from the hall became a focal point in the house.

The last grand period of timbered and panelled staircase design was the Gothic revival of the late 18th and early

Previous page
A steel balustrade and metal landing panel add contemporary detail to a wooden stairway by architect Pierre d'Avoine.
1 & 2 Stairs that look very different from each angle in the ascent by architect Michael Carapettan make best use of minimal space. Diamond-meshed iron risers, which support the reassuringly stolid wooden treads, filter light through the perforations, and bring to a long run an almost transparent quality.

1

2

3

19th centuries. Illuminated by shafts of coloured light refracted through stained-glass window panels, the staircase swept heavenward in imposing splendour. Today, however, with space at a premium, the context for such statements would be quite wrong. Generally, there is no hall and all available space must be freed for living – even the spiral stair requires an area of about 6 feet (2 metres) square to allow for wide, comfortable treads. Prefabricated spiral stairs are designed to telescope upon each tread. This

3 This loft was originally part of an arcade with arches, pilasters and columns. Using the grand height available to him, architect Luigi Ferrario added two platforms in industrial iron grating reached by a ladder-like arrangement of metal stairs.

5

4 & 5 Within this architectural staircase even the landings have been transformed, projecting like diving boards into the lofty space carved out of the interior of this magnificent house. Above the staircase, a glazed roof allows light to fall freely through the perforated mesh variegated grid patterns.

3

3 "Buildings will survive only if driven by ideas" says David Chipperfield, whose innovative staircase frees the risers and treads from panelling. The exposed ascent is flanked by metal flattened into a long handrail. Chipperfield exaggerates the distance between the treads and balustrade in a witty exploitation of scale and proportion.

2

2 Glazing the space between the tubular-steel handrail and the narrow wooden treads on this mild-steel staircase sounds risky, but safety glass is capable of both sustaining assault and holding the light. The staircase was designed by Armstrong Associates for the headquarters of the architectural fittings company Elementer.

1 This detail of the staircase in picture **2** shows how the arched handrail is supported above the glass, protectively enfolding it at the landings.

1

allows them to be easily adjusted, since the positioning of the landing on the first floor will depend on the ceiling height – by no means a standard dimension in older houses that are undergoing renovation.

Spiralling stairs in the 1970s were often taken from old exterior fire escapes, freed of rust and repainted for use in domestic interiors. The spiralling ramps favoured by Frank Lloyd Wright in his Guggenheim Museum in New York, or Frank Gehry in his Vitra Chair Museum in Germany are capable of making possible a gentle ascent for throngs of people, with the added bonus of being suitable for wheelchair access.

In the contemporary home, however, design features such as these take up too much space. Mass-produced lines are adjusted in scale to account for reduced ceiling heights and the lack of space for landings, while the best staircases are still custom-built on site using prefabricated parts. Aluminium

4

4 The owners of this custom-built staircase by the inventive Ron Arad of One Off call it "a steel waterfall". The house was built in the 1850s, but was gutted and then custom-designed for the current owners. For example, both are very tall, and this staircase paces the treads accordingly.

5

5 Without the central fireman's pole, a spiral staircase takes a twist in form from Dimes, using the "Modula" black metal backbone to support the treads.

6

6 "PV4" is a modular handrail, ribbed in anti-slip black rubber. It is made by Dimes and can be paired with a range of staircase components, including the "PG500".

11

7 Hewi modular handrail systems produce corner designs, angled balustrades, connections and end fittings designed to hold securely clear protective acrylic sheets. Rails are in nylon with a steel core – a strong, easy-to-clean material that is never too hot or cold to the touch and which is non-conductive to electricity or static charges.

8 & 9 Steel braces clip together like a child's toy to make a self-supporting staircase angled for any twist or turn. Albini and Fontanot mass-produce Roberto Molinazzi's design in polyurethaned steel. Geometric line and well-studied proportions accentuate the scale of the staircase.

treads snake along a gradual incline, as rigorously pleated as an origami cut, uncluttered by finicky balustrades, since the wall acts as the backdrop. The effect is theatrical – an unbroken line like a caterpillar uncoiled. On a practical level, it intrudes very little into the room below and provides the viewer with an interesting profile. The concept is based on Palladio's flying staircase in the Academy, Venice, which spirals upward without any visible support other than the bonding of the steps into the outer wall.

Another neat architectural trick to take the eye visually upward and apparently lengthen rooms with low ceilings and meanly proportioned staircases, is to double the length between treads. This gives the appearance of elongating the ascent without actually taking up any additional space. This "visual stretch" is often used by the architect Pierre d'Avoine to make a narrow studio – even one just 10 feet (3 metres) across,

10 Dimes produce stairs that fold, spiral, or fit together in modular pieces. This versatility means that Dimes components will create a staircase to fit most spaces. Shown here is their metal-cast spiral model, the "PG 500", which is polyurethaned in scarlet, with its fan-like treads lined in rubber or carpet. It can be matched with a variety of handrails, like the "PV4" (see **6** above).

11 Architect Rick Mather achieved a staircase of Hollywood grandeur, with curves like a Cresta run and handrails that resolve their angular differences in a clever cross-over of a quarter turn with winders, to front the entrance to this top-floor studio apartment.

8

7

9

10

81

1 An unfurled ribbon of steel extended from the top of this office by architects Von Gerkan, Marg and partner provides an airy, deceptively lightweight, open staircase with flattened handrails attenuated as finely as tagliatelle.

2 Narrow steel treads, evenly paced with a fine, nonslip carpet lining, are given a curved edge on one side of the staircase, known as the nosing. Architect Lustig has made full use of illumination in this space by backlighting the sloping back projection that follows the incline of the stairs.

4 Albini and Fontanot's narrow 3/4-inch (2-cm) diameter hand-rail is made of metal treated with resinous polyurethane. The handrail can be conveniently attached to any balusters from the newel, or principal post, found at the foot of the stairs.

5 Colin Gold of Aukett Associates has brought neo-classical flourishes to the plain geometry of this mahogany-stained staircase, with its steel ziggurat bannisters, which links an upper studio with the lower-floor kitchen.

6 Downtrodden winders rarely get a decorative treatment, though with a spiral staircase very often the view from below is of these wedges wending their way upward. The solution from architects Tsao and Mckown is to splay these fan-shaped, ribbed treads within a well of light so that they cast a pattern on the floor below.

3 Though all but impossible for a modern architect to build himself a new house in central London, Sir Richard Rogers, Britain's most fashionable architect, carved out a contemporary interior for himself by combining two 19th-century houses. Where there were six rooms, now the dazzling space has a galleried bedroom floor reached via a dramatic, perforated stainless steel staircase and, above, this suspended ladder walkway on the top landing. The flapped theatrical lights battened to the landing cast light down the large distances covered.

wall to wall – appear less confined. Safety is a vital factor when planning stairs, but one of the unusual aspects of stair design is to use an unexpected material of the correct tensile strength. The stair treads here, for example, can be disquieting, yet they are made from safety glass laid like slats on iron supports. Today the laser cutter can shape glass in many superior ways, losing sharp edges altogether.

Freedom from timber technology, alongside a more controlled spatial manipulation as living spaces shrink, produces dramatic ascents, with staircases that are not even encased but sculptural walkways that slice through space, turning corners precipitously at the same time as they open up the view. Other senses, as well as the visual, are challenged. The British architect and designer

7 Looking up through a steel mesh platform, architect David Wild's staircase sets the honeyed colour of wooden treads against black tubular-steel handrails and silvery steel uprights.

8 Albini and Fontanot delineate with a spindly lineup of balusters the gracious curve of their matte-black, high-tech staircase, "Xnodo".

9 The "Stonington Stair" in steel with cherry-wood risers and treads, by McBride and Horowitz, is a good resolution of a modern staircase in a 200-year-old salt-box house in New England. Its sculptural simplicity echoes the puritan spirit and rigorous functionalism of the original architecture.

3 & 4 Riverside ware-houses, while providing spectacular views and large rooms, are notoriously difficult to convert to living space. Architect John Young fitted a vertebraed, yellow, buttressed staircase with slatted teak treads on rollerball bearings so that it can be swivelled around to take advantage of the vast floor space. The staircase's lightweight mobility and structural strength makes it as flexible as airport landing steps. The steel gangplank leads to a bedroom on a concrete platform supported by steel rods suspended from the roof.

1 In this house, the wooden treads and landing are parquet for a superior finish. Wooden staircases were traditionally built to the standard quarter-turn or dogleg pattern, employing lathe-turned newels, risers, treads and balusters. Since the Industrial Revolution and the relative ease with which cast-iron or mild steel can be made into staircase components, the mass-produced wooden staircase has become a dull reproduction piece reduced in size to fit today's rooms. The best contemporary wooden staircases are those which expose the treads like vertebrae, elevating the planks of solid wood visually and simply in a free-standing staircase.

2 In this staircase, by Albini and Fontanot, laminated beech or walnut wooden risers fan out from a central wooden newel post. The result, a staircase that takes up the least possible floor space.

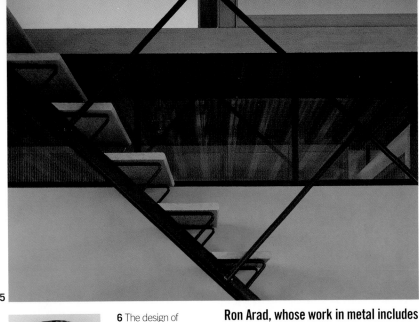

5 The background to stairs can make a standard run appear more dramatic, as architect David Wild proves in painting this ascent midnight blue. The vivid colour stands out against the mellowed tones of wooden treads attached to black metal risers.

6 The design of the spiral is important when the interior has not been revamped as open, flowing space. Here, refurbishment was limited to the standard little well between the floors, where the meanly proportioned old stairs once ran. The solution, the "L 20" by Dimes, pays tribute to its Bauhaus origins in the style that harks back to Walter Gropius and his 1914 designs.

7 When only occasional access is required – to a roof terrace in this case – space-saving designs like this flat steel staircase with oak treads, by David Chipperfield, can be brought into play. The central metal pole serves both as support and handrail.

Ron Arad, whose work in metal includes voluminous stainless steel sofas and chairs, made the staircase in his original shop, which was appropriately named One Off, in London's Covent Garden. The staircase was formed from giant timbers wired to a Moog synthesizer. Everybody walking or rushing along these stairs made their own rhythmic music with each footfall. Arad's first commissioned staircase in a house was made from two continuous strips of metal crossing each other at right-angles to form rectangular picture frame shapes when seen in profile. The stair rail was a single sweep of metal curving like a bow across the structure, which has been described as a "steel waterfall".

You can make simpler staircases of course, using iron building brackets supporting metal mesh treads, or mahogany steps buttressed to joists without bannisters. Sometimes the winder, a tread wider at one end than the other, starts off the staircase ascent and leads the climber upward.

Newel posts, the principal posts at the ends of a flight of steps that support **7**

1

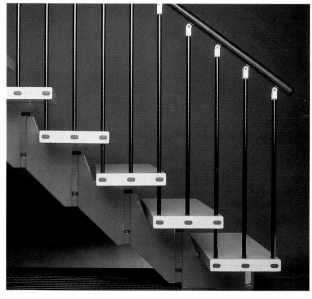

2

1 Beech is the silky smooth wood favoured for "Parisienne", the spiral staircase by Dimes which evokes Art Deco style. When different flights of stairs are not in the same line, the change of direction is achieved either by landings or, as here, by winders. Winders are steps, the treads of which taper for left or right turns. By contrast, landings are constructed as small floors and may be either half or three-quarter landings according to the angle between flights.

2 Laminated beech or walnut treads, protected by a transparent veneer, fit on a central metal support in red, blue or black. Made by Albini and Fontanot, and designed by Molinazzi from Index-studio, Milan, each tread is pierced by balustrades in primary colours.

3

4

5

4 & 5 Peter Wilson, working with Chassay Wright, created a private gallery above an office. The gallery is reached by an open stairwell with a balustrade forming a slinky seat, as if a giant dragonfly had alighted on the wall. The curve in the balustrade above it echoes the point at which the sitter can relax.

the handrail, can be in contrasting material, such as steel with wooden treads, or vice versa. Pierre d'Avoine believes it is important to have a rough-hewn honesty to stair rails in cramped, modern spaces, that same quality Hawksmoor sought with his lathe-turned posts on lectern stairs.

The ironwork traditionally used for balustrades at street level presents the designer with an opportunity for splendid neo-baroque flourishes or more practical uses. One example of such an application is a staircase by architect Pierre d'Avoine, a swooping lectern

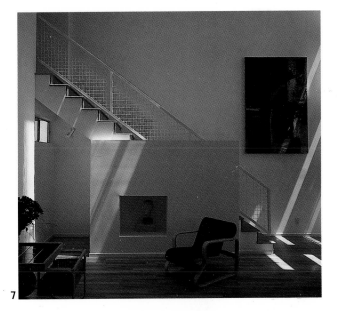

7

3 A central stairwell is evenly paced by Gwathmey Siegel in American hardwood. The staircase begins with two flights meeting at a central ascent and then bifurcates to serve two separate wings on the landing.

6

6 This cherrywood staircase at the end of a combined eat-in kitchen/ dining area is by architect David Chipperfield. It brings a clarity of light and variety of tone within a simple structure in this tiny house.

7 Strands of twisted wire marshalled between steel joists, painted pastel yellow, form an unusual barrier for these simple wooden stairs, framed by a large, white display base, in a scheme by architect Frank Fitzgibbons.

STAIRS

1 Engineering feats are possible with reinforced concrete, which allows a more fluid ascent than either wood or stone. Within a corner, a sweep of stairs curves upward with balustrades in five bands of tubular steel to follow the twist like music sheets.

2 Stair treads are often viewed from the back, which in a triangular stacking exercise leads to boring uniformity. But this ascent of moulded stairs, each cast individually and arranged with little overlap, makes a feature of the risers.

3, 4 & 5 A reminder that humble concrete is the sculptor's medium is seen here, in a design by architect Charles van den Hove. Double stairs within a central stairwell frame a blond wood door on the first landing. The handrail that swoops above the stairs replicates their oval form. On the handrails, epoxyed to resemble antique pewter, the capping piece on which the hand rests when ascending or descending the stairs is usually rounded like this, and fixed about 2 feet 6 inches (0.75 metre) above the line of the nosing. The opposite view from the front doorway is toward the dining room and the open space of the garden beyond.

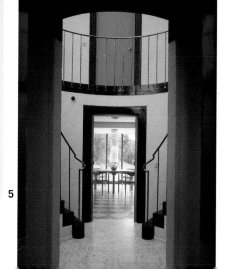

6 From Cecilia and Ottorino Berselli comes an example of rigorous straightline geometry. Their whitewashed concrete stairs are given a silvered lining with marbled veneers on the treads, set in relief against a natural stone and mortared wall. Designed for a house in Italy, traditional local materials are used in a contemporary way.

6

attached to the bannisters on the landings – thereby improvizing a small reading space in a tiny house.

Cunningly exploiting the sheer narrowness of the rooms and their lack of height, these structures in geometric configurations have handsome safety features, such as an overscaled handrail in marble. Architect David Chipperfield used this as a method of enticing the newcomer to look beyond

7 Simple precast concrete forms unravel like a helter-skelter course on precipitous curves supporting generous treads, evenly paced, covered along their entire width in elephant-grey carpet. Few verticals delineate this spectacular piece of engineering by Rick Mather, who illuminates his design with natural light from a glazed roof panel above the stairwell.

7

the cramped entrance to the studio upstairs. Scaled more appropriately for a hotel lobby, he set his gigantic, grey-marbled handrail against a cavernous main wall to create a real flight of fancy in a simple setting.

Stairs are more than just a means of getting between levels, according to Japanese architect Ryoji Suzuki they are "a device which obliquely traverses space". Slicing diagonally across interiors with stone, wood or steel mesh treads supported on tubular steel columns or rigid rigging, contemporary architects produce designs for staircases that are dramatic to look at, yet safe as houses.

1 & 2 In his dramatic black staircase, Albert Bardawil emphasizes the turns it takes by lining the concrete stairs with black

travertine. The balustrade is a flat black metal twist. The space in Bardawil's apartment was so restricted that he commissioned

a structural engineer to work out the exact dimensions required for his staircase.

3 Ron Arad's original London shop, One Off, featured this staircase cast in concrete with wooden railroad-sleeper treads wired to a Moog synthesizer so that each footfall created its own music. The guard rail, in mild tempered steel, blow torched with patterns by Arad, also served as a loud-speaker for the staircase synthesizer.

4 A narrow concrete staircase beneath a bricked vaulted ceiling is open on one side in the Mediterranean style. Architect David

Chipperfield accentuates this imagery with blue sliding doors and panels and a cobalt coloured tubular-steel frame.

7 Western in appearance, Eastern in spirit, Tadao Ando's buildings in Japan are stark and spare but also refined and serene.

6 Stolid stairs washed in midnight blue are lit all the time by low lighting in grid panels by Luxo, throwing a shaft of pyramidal light. Luxo believe that it is vital that nightlights stay on a low dimmer for staircase safety.

5 These stairs, on the 24th floor of an old mansion block, lead to a breathtaking viewing spot. Architect Steven Forman chose a

stainless steel handrail above carpeted stone stairs to connect all three levels. Vertical "light troughs" run the length of the stairs.

Heating

When the French celebrity designer Philippe Starck brandishes his firedogs and pokers designed for New York's fashionable hotel, the Century Paramount, and puts them into mass production, it is time to sit up and notice that the humble, and sometimes obsolete, hearth is getting the designer treatment.

After centuries of fulfilling general household and cooking needs, the fireplace is now banned in smokeless zones, or glows artificially with fake logs and pine spray that simply reinforce the illusion that the fire is really gas-fed. Central heating has brought about the changes in our attitude to what was formerly the focal point of the home—the fireplace. Nowadays, heat is beamed into our homes in three ways: directly as rays from the sun or the blaze from the fire; convected with warm-air currents circulated by a fan heater; and conducted as in direct contact, like the heat from an electric blanket.

The Romans, who were first with many

1 Believing modernists were ill-served by standard domestic fittings, Mark Marcinik set up design company Next to M. Their fire surround is constructed of oak, plywood and galvanized steel, and incorporates a bar and firewood-storage facility.

Previous page In architect John Young's penthouse the underfloor heating system is supplemented by wall-mounted, industrial heating elements from the Tranter Corporation. These take the form of stainless steel platecoils, ranged in tiers like rows of Samurai shields.
2 A semi-cylindrical, rendered brick fireplace provides the focal point in a large galleried room by Gwathmey Siegel. The central hearth, flanked by storage recesses for logs, is screened with wire-mesh safety curtains.
3 Commissioned by architect Charles Jencks, designer Michael Graves and sculptor Celia Scott conceived this fireplace on a monumental scale. Constructed of MDF, the fluted posts and lintel, and column above, have been marbled to convey solidity and enhance classical references in the design.

4 Sculptural column radiators, such as this black, strip-panelled model in architect Michael Russum's apartment, accent the distinctive lines of the surrounding architecture, rather than fade anonymously into the background.

5 From the Platonic Fireplace Company, a gas-fired and geometrically inspired fireplace comprising a fire surround of marbled spheres, tetrahydrons, cones, cylinders and cubes, and a chrome-finished steel "Plato" grate housing high-heat ceramic "Geologs".

6 Designed by Arbonia and distributed by Bisque, the sinuous X-stream radiator turns a functional device into a piece of domestic sculpture. It stands 75 inches (1.90 m) tall and is available in more than 1500 stove-enamelled colours, or plated in brass, nickel, chrome or gold.

architectural innovations, had under-floor heating installed in the city of Bath in England in AD60, where they piped hot spa water in underground pipes throughout the interiors of their buildings. Today's underfloor hot-water systems do not rely on spas; the water is heated by gas-, oil-, coal- or wood-burning boilers, or solar panels and heat pumps.

Skirting and underfloor heating systems have been popular in the United States for many years and they are now catching on in Germany. These concealed systems are the most unobtrusive method of heating in the architectural interior. Skirting radiators emit heat all around the room and are nearly invisible, thus imposing no restrictions on the placement of radiator panels, entrances or furniture.

One stage further, without even skirting boards, which most late-modernists eschew, there are underfloor heating

3 "Acostyle" from Runtal is assembled from four blocks of slatted panels, available in various sizes and heated by either hot water or electric filaments.
4 Aluminium flooring is an ideal heat conductor for this gas-fired "Radia-Vector" by Zehnder, in Jan Kaplicky's apartment conversion in a 19th-century city house.
5 "Griglia", a 30-bar grid radiator from Runtal, which runs on one-fifth of the hot water required to heat a conventional radiator, can also be used to partition a room.

6 The "Ideal Elan 2", a wall-mounted, gas-fired radiator panel from Stelrad, can be unobtrusively inserted into a run of kitchen cabinets.

1 Usually concealed in the walls, the plumbing is revealed in this copper piping towel rail from Butler and Radice.
2 A towel rail, ladder radiators and classic radiator by Arbonia, all chromed and the latter available to order, curved or angled, floor- or wall-mounted.

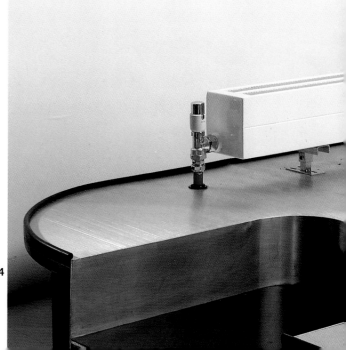

7 Classic, concertina-style, Clyde combustion radiators run on the gas boiler system and are bolted together on site to the required length. Architect David Chipperfield, who favours the industrial appearance of these chunky units, has placed them near the windows of this small studio house to maximize convection.

7

8 Floor-mounted, the short, squat Runtal "Reflex" radiator is the ideal size and shape for installing beneath windows in order to make best use of convection currents.

9 Stelrad Ideal's "Accord" central heating, gas-fired panel radiators, by Caradon, are available in a wide range of sizes and are notable for their plainly tailored simplicity.

8

10 The "Sculptur" curved towel rail from Zehnder can be supplied with an optional electric immersion heater to make it independent of the central heating system and operative all year around. Never install the system on open circuits or underfloor systems.

10

systems that warm the entire surface area of the floor. Every other heating system depends on convectional currents to disperse the heat around the room, rising as hot air always does. In high-ceilinged rooms, this can mean cold corners and chilly surfaces.

Underfloor heating systems run at surprisingly low temperatures, less than blood heat, which allows you to use a wide range of flooring finishes, even wood, without risk of damage or warping. These finishes can be laid on the original concrete base, on an already screeded floor as well as on a suspended board one.

Low-temperature, radiant heat, rather than the much higher, hot-air temperature type, can come from radiators hidden behind the narrowest and slimmest of skirting boards, or from slender panels that are a mere 5 inches

9

12

11 Made to be recessed in small, low room spaces, the Runtal "Convettore" functions at pre-set temperatures. When sited beneath a plate-glass window, the stainless steel radiator body appears to double up as a skirting board.

12 The "King" radiator from Runtal was designed by Paul Priestman to look like a tall, cylindrical torch. It is manufactured in naturally anodized aluminium.

13 The "JeT X" (model HX) by Runtal, is a wall-mounted, strip-panelled radiator.

1 Runtal's wall-mounted tubular "Acovex" radiators run off the hot water systems in bathrooms or kitchens.
2 Wall-mounted column radiators from Runtal's "Scaldasalviette" range are available in various dimensions to suit most room sizes.

3 A modern interior which makes a virtue of contemporary fittings, rather than trying to hide them. The radiator panel, loudspeaker, window blind, Eileen Gray chrome table and vase and flowers are assembled to create a pleasing still life out of everyday modern elements.

4 Radiant crystal, pioneered by micro-wave ovenware and used for hobs and cooktops for years, has made its way into this innovatory wall-mounted heater panel, the "Omeglass", from Runtal.

5 Chrome "Classic", white panel and red and yellow "Crea-Therm" radiators by Arbonia prove that radiators need not be utility objects. Distributors Bisque claim the range is "heating art".

(12.5 cm) high and placed above existing skirting boards.

If you intend to use direct heat dependent on a fireplace, then you need to pay careful attention to detail to ensure that the most energy is conserved. Glass-fronted fires and enclosed stoves are considerably more efficient than open-fronted fires. Some of the most energy-conserving offer 80 percent efficiency, which allows them to take over as the primary source of heat rather than acting as a top-up to a radiator system. A damper fitted to the chimney will narrow the flue and control the flow of air that causes hot air to rush up the chimney to the outside.

Modern fireplaces have a dog-grate with a hood, looking much like a kitchen ventilator above the oven, or else the free-standing fire has a modern flue lining over the wider old

6 An electric fan heater designed to be built into the plinth under kitchen cabinets and save valuable floor space. Controls are located on the work surface, and there is a cool air setting for summer.

7 The "Chorus" radiator by Marimex, with six slats on a shallow radiator panel, has a distinctive yet unobtrusive presence in this light-filled corner.
8 Industrial radiator ducts, originally concealed under steel fascia, are stripped to reveal their slinky coils in architect Ben Kelly's factory conversion.

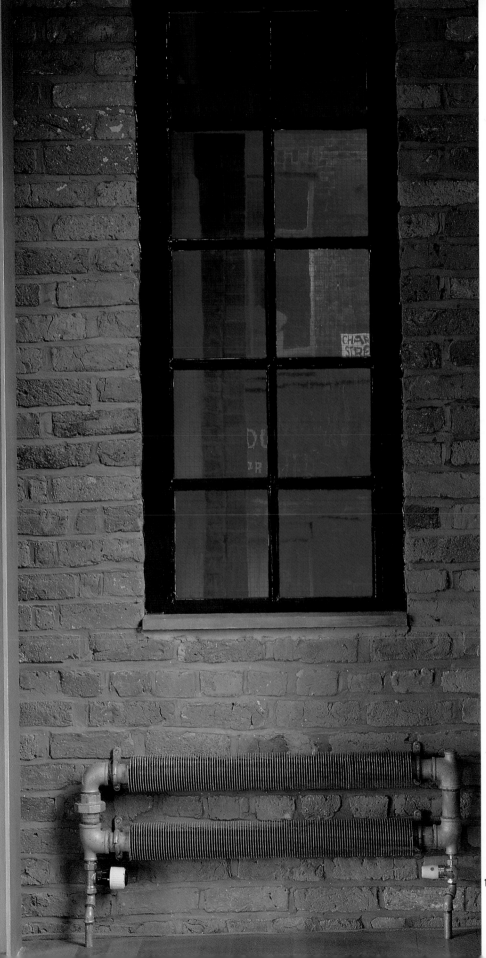

flue to connect with the hood. Channels around the fire casing heat the air drawn toward the fire and recycle it to warm the room, producing nearly twice the heat of an ordinary flame-effect fire for the same input of gas. A fireplace is not just a pretty face or, indeed, the visual focal point of a room. If our planet is to survive, we need to address the basic problems of heating and room insulation effectively, since both of them have a dramatic effect on overall energy consumption.

Before the advent of scientific combustion theories, houses were buffered against the cold with tapestries, wall-hangings, porches, panelling and window shutters. These types of decoration have no place in the modern interior. In their place, the strictures – and structures – for engineering must reside with the heating specialist and the homeowner. For example, in Britain the domestic market accounts for

9

9 Marimex's "Novella Bains" laddered towel rail in bright scarlet adds a jolt of bold colour to a white bathroom.
10 Because this free-standing Zehnder radiator runs on low-temperature oil- or gas-fired systems, it can safely double up as a partition wall.

10

11

11 These colourful and robust multi-columned "Classic" radiators from Zehnder run economically on low-temperature heating systems, and come in more than 100 listed sizes to fit almost any space.

1 Abundant space and light in a villa by architect Jo Crepain provide the perfect background for the uncompromising functionalism of a classic, cast-iron, wood-burning stove.

2 A prototype for a cast-iron, wood-burning stove by Benn Gurleyik has ridged and stippled sides to increase the surface area and so maximize the convection of heat.

1

3 "Gyrofocus" by Atelier Dominique, ingeniously suspended from the flue, highlights the sculptural potential in fireplace design, for too long anchored to the hearth. The ensemble is finished in a high-heat-resistant, matte-black coating.

4 Made by Piazzetta, the "Romeo" wood-burning stove features a glazed pottery casing that convects heat from a cast-iron firebox.

4

3

5 Most wood-burning stoves are given a pseudo-antique casing, but the "Seneca" from Vermont Castings has been designed for contemporary interiors. It also burns clean to meet the stringent requirements of the American Environmental Protection Agency.

5

almost 50 percent of the energy used in the country. Consumer awareness can affect regulations as well as manufacturers' products, and awareness of energy-saving, though yawningly dull when presented in therms, can make the difference between running an efficient, economic home and a casual but expensive one.

Thus far, only the fireplace surround, that consummate piece of ornate framing to the glow within, has been neglected in the design treatment. On the whole, products made today are arrested in a time warp with Adam

6 Solid-fuel-burning stoves are architects' favourites for homes equipped with a coal or wood bunker, since their industrial shape and functional form make them a focal point. Since heat rises, freeing the flue of a wood-burning stove to act like a tubular radiator on the floor above will save energy. David Wild protects surrounding surfaces by inserting a marble fire surround and hearth.

carved surrounds clustered with cheaply moulded and glued-on cornucopias, or perhaps Louis Quinze marble veneers. Fireplaces are period pieces, and the clean lines and fresh designs of the modern fireplace few and far between. Perhaps it is a reflection of the fact that in the last 20 years flues have not been built into modern homes. Now there is a realization that every home needs an open flue, since it provides natural ventilation that keeps the air fresh at the same time as it removes water vapour in the air. One of the main causes of damp in temperate climates is condensation, which occurs not solely because walls are poorly insulated, but also because damp air without a natural escape route condenses on all cold surfaces.

One important contemporary detail to have emerged in the last ten years as a functional heating system and stolid focal point is the kitchen range.

6

9

7

8

Central-heating cookers or ranges, which have been regarded as standard equipment in French, Swiss and German farmhouses for a century, have been updated to heat back boilers that hold water for baths, and pump it around a system of radiators extensive enough for the requirements of a four-bedroomed home. You no longer need a farmhouse, and a coal bunker or woodshed, to support one of these ranges, since modern ones can happily run on oil, gas or electricity.

Solid fuel, for years in the doldrums, has received a better press, especially

7 The hexagonal-shaped "Brooklyn" from Thermocet runs on natural or propane gas to give a coal-fire effect when viewed through the angled safety-glass front..

8 Thermocet's handsome "Elite Focus" free-standing stove combines a pressed steel canopy and hearth unit with an "Elite 7000" Prima convector, with flame effect. It runs on natural or propane gas to give a 4.8kW output.

9 Sited on a ceramic tiled hearth, the stainless steel coal-burning stove becomes the focal point of David Wild's interior.

1 A prismatic wall fitting in fireproof glass, the "Visiofocus 900" by Atelier Dominique features a completely visible hearth that slots into a space 36 inches (91 cm) high and 39 inches (99 cm) wide.

2 "Leina", a stylish set of stainless steel firetongs designed by Pep Bonet for Alessi, brings state-of-the-art accessorizing to the formerly much-neglected hearth.

since the larger ash cans need emptying only once a week. Also, smokeless fuels and modern fireplaces get fires burning quicker, and the industry has poured money into designs that take advantage of these innovations to ensure that once more fireplaces are burning brightly as focal points in modern rooms.

One of the great advantages of central heating is that it freed the home from electric heaters, wood-burning stoves and gas fires, and all the consequent cords and clutter needed to fuel and tend the system. Remarkably realistic gas-log and gas-coal fires have made many of the accessories for the fire obsolete, yet designers still tackle the task of welding weird shapes for grates, fender stools, log holders and fire doors for those contemporary homes where coal is still king.

As architects try to reconcile themselves to the battery of equipment that central heating requires, perversely they still choose the unimaginative corrugated radiators. These giant industrial cylinders are the old war-horses of an ancient regime, yet they seem infinitely preferred for their unrelenting presence than the newer, slimmer, pared-down versions in plain white. Thermostatic controls on every radiator make heat output adjustable and, in larger houses, the radiator circuits for each floor are separated so that the thermostat and timer controls operate independently. The flat-faced designs that avoid the clumsy joints with pipe

3 Marble fire surrounds usually follow traditional patterns, but this one breaks the mould. And the unusual effect is enhanced by the halved ziggurats in glass and travertine on the mantel.

4 The "Dovre 2000" fireplace system incorporates folding glass doors which can be closed to allow wood or solid fuel to burn safely and economically overnight.

5 The inglenook fireplace dates back to Tudor times and incorporated a seat or bench beside or within the chimney breast. This contemporary version by architect Frank Fitzgibbons provides ample seating (and reading material) on a zig-zagging platform.

---

8 Elgin and Hall's reproduction of a Louis XV fluted pedestal, negra marble fire surround – the "Louis Petite" – is proof that period pieces can be dramatic in a modern setting. Originally conceived for Louis' state rooms, this is one of the most enduring of all fire surround designs.

9 "Tito Lucifer" fire-dogs are a striking feature of the fireplaces designed by Philippe Starck for the Royalton Hotel, New York. Their classic horn shape became Starck's *leitmotif* throughout the Royalton project. They were put into production by OWO.

10 Starck's designs for the Royalton are a fine example of how traditional methods of heating can be successfully integrated into a modern interior.

connections at their bottom edge, the Swiss Zehnder ladder towel radiators and the adventurous models with curvaceous pipes in the shape of a giant X are some of the flamboyant newcomers to the radiator scene.

Many architects still cling to the belief that radiators are best placed beneath windows, since the cold night air is counteracted by the warm air rising from the radiators. Just as fireplaces are best positioned centrally, so, too, should radiators be placed around the internal walls. Their form and colour can then be used to decorative effect. After all, period-piece restorers have traditionally been hard put to cut out of their scheme the essential central-heating radiator, and instead camouflage it behind ridiculous trellis frames. So why not draw attention to the hearth and heart of the modern building? 10

6 In an interior combining curves and right angles, the unusual corner viewing window to the firebox has been cleverly accentuated by a semi-circular sweep of marble below the hearth.

7 The traditional combination of built-in hearth and flue, decorative mantelpiece of wood, brick, stone or marble, and overmantel mirror above, is given a stylish modern twist by Lighthouse Interiors. Flanking light-box columns augment the blaze in the hearth and refract light into the room – an effect accentuated by the glass shelf above.

1 Frank Fitzgibbons makes an architectural feature out of a necessity with a scarlet exterior chimney flue dramatically visible through the glazing above the fireplace.

2 The Hursley fireplace from Dimplex incorporates an electric, real flame effect "Optiflame" heater, compatible with six other designs from their range.

3 An elegant *pare feu* (firescreen) from Avant Scene's "Terrazzo" range. It co-ordinates with the tongs and poker illustrated in picture **7**.

4 The Platonic Fireplace Company's gas-fired "Socrates" incorporates ceramic geologs and variable flame controls.

5 Fires that draw well depend as much upon the shape of the design as the convection of the flue behind. Philip Hearsey's handsome stone-surround fireplace incorporates a spacious hearth and an appropriately generous storage recess for logs.

6 Designer Philip Hearsey, working with blacksmith Peter Smith, often uses salvaged metal – specifically chosen for its "inimitable" naturally worn and weathered surface texture – to create the individual firebacks, hoods, tools and fire-baskets in his "Radnor" range.

7 "Pince" and "Soufflet" (tongs and poker), are from Avant Scene's "Terrazzo" range, which was created in a "new spirit to present the objects and furniture of young designers and sculptors".

Lighting

Technological innovation has moved the concept of lighting a long way from the point where lights were no more than openings between the mullions of a window. The first electric lights were modelled on, or converted from, gas lamps or candle holders. Even today, many light fittings still show their origin in the chandelier or candlestick. By the 1970s an alternative had reached the mass market—batteries of spotlights marshalled on tracks across the ceiling. However, the heat and size of tungsten bulbs proved to be a drawback for designers.

Today, electricity is seen by many as the most potent force in design and architecture. The invention of low-voltage lights, first called "sealed reflector lamps", in 1972, brought about a revolution in lighting design because this new system miniaturized the source, while giving it tighter optical control. The new generation of low-voltage tungsten or metal-halide lights are capable of bathing a wall in light, highlighting any chosen area, and washing objects in

Previous page Crystal horn-shaped lights, "Lucefair", designed by Philippe Starck for the Royalton Hotel, New York, are available for the domestic market from Flos.
1 Stephan Copeland's gooseneck "Tango" table lamp in aluminium, houses a single 50W 12V quartz-halogen bulb.
2 De Pas, D'Urbino and Lomazzi's ceiling lamp, "Nessie", in lacquered or anodized metal for Stilnovo houses five dichroic bulbs.
3 Alberto Fraser designed "Nastro" for Stilnovo. Multicoloured computer straps support the halogen head, and a friendly "mouse" is the transformer and switch.

1

2

3

4 Battened onto the scaffolded, galleried floor in Sir Richard Rogers' home are two enormous theatrical lights, with flaps and reflectors to harness the beams. No single light source is better than another – it depends on the functions and positioning of the lamps.

4

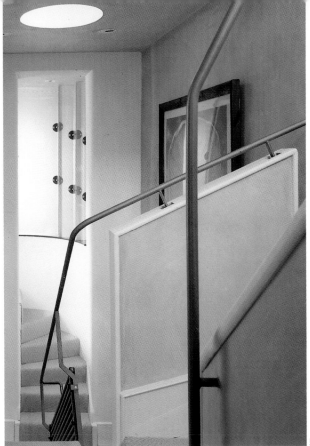

5 In this apartment designed by Munkenbeck & Marshall, a pool of opaque light is beamed down from the ceiling. This low-level lighting is reinforced with a ring of low-voltage downlighters, their transformers hidden in the ceiling, and their small, intense beams diffused by the more general, centrally positioned light.

6 A modern classic fitting from Woka Lamps' Art Collection series. "Spectrum" is made in a contemporary material – acrylic glass – and was designed by Mathias Pfeffer.

7 Oil lamp and candlestick imagery for lamps prevailed until the 1920s, when Mario Fortuny first housed a 500W bulb in a photographer's cast-iron studio fitting. It is still made today by Ecart International.

8 "Titania" from Luceplan suspends a halogen bulb from steel cables. It is screened by an elliptical shade that changes colour according to rib-like filters. Designers are Alberto Meda and Paolo Rizzato.

LIGHTING

1 Dean Wang installed a line of uplighters in the floor to wash the wall in light where it was most needed. The lights are sealed with shatter-proof glass.

2 A lighting layout for concealed or recessed fittings has to be planned by an architect or electrician ahead of decoration.

3 Most concealed and recessed fixtures are inflexibly positioned in the ceiling or floor. So iGuzzini's development of an adjustable downlighter whose beam can swivel is an innovative approach. The "Pixel" model, which is available in two sizes, uses different types of lamp.

4 & 5 "I hate ceiling lights," says architect John Pawson, who always uses floor lights fitted with tungsten-halogen sources for an intense white beam from small fittings. The transformer that converts the mains voltage is concealed under the oak floorboards.

6 "Myriad" low-voltage downlighters from Concord now include a dichroic version accepting "True-Aim" sealed-beam lamps.

6

7

7 "Equinox", Concord's versatile range of cone downlighters, includes the recently developed elliptical metal-halide 100W lamp.

8 Ceilingward glances will spot the unobtrusive ring frame harnessing the white light of tungsten halogen in Concord's "Chorus".

warm golden or silvery light, depending on the reflector being used.

Contemporary lighting systems can also help to structurally enhance an interior. For example, an architect can isolate solid walls of storage shelving by bathing the wall above and below the system with light from the new miniaturized fluorescent tubes. Slimmed down by Philips for use in supermarkets, these tubes are capable of creating an icy white light that, concealed behind battens, floods the wall with brightness and thus helps to reduce the visual impact of the massed volume of a library of bookshelves.

Lighting design is a question of balance between the quality of light and of shadows. Too much light is too obvious –diffusion, not glare, is the object. So it is hardly surprising that the dramatic spotlit effects in schemes by architects such as Philippe Starck use the same overhead system as theatre designers – banked spotlights. From compact fluorescents to metal halides, from incandescent to low-voltage halogen, phosphor and high-pressure discharge lamps, spotlight fittings are strung up

8

9 Lighting can brighten or soften, dramatize or minimize. In a darker room, reflective light is reduced, so there are usually more light sources to compensate.

9

10 Fittings are less important than the quality of light they shed, as these unobtrusive wall and ceiling lights from the architectural team of Stanton Williams for the Issey Miyake shop highlight.

11 Ideas borrowed from commercial fittings have validity at home, just as theatrical lenses and beams are now making their way into domestic fittings. Overhead background lighting will wash a wall with light.

10

11

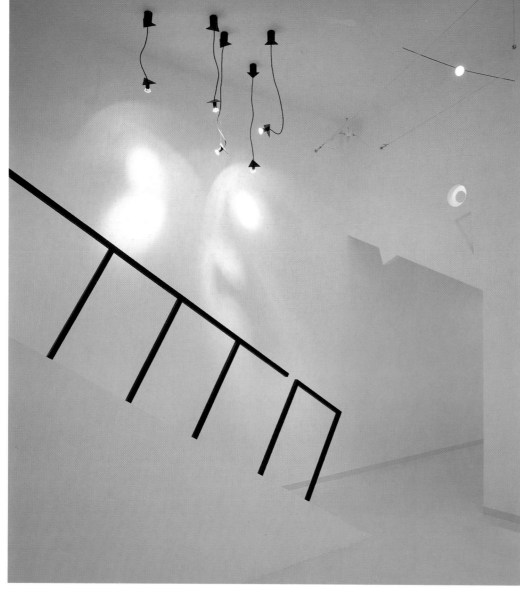

1 The miniaturization of light sources has encouraged the design of playful fittings in which to house them – unlike the earnest track systems of 20 years ago. This record store is highlighted by neo-baroque spots suspended from tentacled arms over the ceiling.

4 Concord's lighting concept, "Infinite", by Woodgate and Lawrence extends the frontiers of conventional track systems. Components screw together, doing away with visible wiring from the transformer.

4

5

5 With "Infinite" (see picture 4), because spotlights can be attached above and below the track or, using the extension power rods, at a distance from the track, unusual features are easy to highlight.

alongside each other, with shields, reflectors and coloured glass discs to change angle and widen or colour the beam of light. Fresnel lenses, named after the French physicist Fresnel, soften the edges of shafts of light on these technical lighting systems (they were originally designed for showrooms and exhibitions, but made the crossover into the home).

The range and complexity of contemporary lighting is daunting to the non-professional – wonderful effects can be achieved, but often not without specialist advice, as well as an electrician's help. For example, you can create a ceiling studded with prismatic light by building in a selection of downlighters – recessed tungsten downlights and eyeball spotlights. Not unexpectedly, this technical talk serves to take the medium further away from the amateur,

2 Like its namesake, the "Shuttle" spotlight for iGuzzini by Bruno Gecchelin sheds sections and casings as required. With this system, there are different shields and reflectors that fit onto a cylinder that houses 22 varieties of lamp. With different accessories, the beam becomes a thread, a blade or a sea of light.

3 Projector lights by Erco, from the "Emanon" range, which was developed with Roy Fleetwood. They are high-performance units that are characterized by multiple light, colour and projection effects, which all reflect the growing domestic interest in theatrical lighting.

3

7

1

6 A variety of spotlights are available for Concord's "Infinite", including a 20W capsule (smaller unit) and a 50W capsule (larger unit). The track and spotlights are available in either black or white.

7 Positioned above steel storage units, powerful spotlights beam light into architect John Young's apartment. On the desk, the low-voltage task light is made by Artemide and is entitled "Berenice".

8 & 9 Two views of the uncompromisingly stylish "Tijuca" from the talented designer Ingo Maurer, who says: "My idea was to create a light that flies like a bird. A light that dances, glides, tilts, balances, rotates." Its main innovative feature is the freely sliding ring connecting the lighting elements to the cables. The ring conducts the current and makes it possible to turn the lighting element through 360° and to move it up or down through 140°.

but it is worth seeking out expert advice or literature because good lighting is the most unobtrusive and effective detail you can bring into your home. However, partly as a result of its technical mysteries, lighting is the most undervalued commodity in the contemporary interior. No one visiting the latest apartment makeover in a gloomy New York brownstone would realize how dingy and dark and Dickensian that space would seem to be without contemporary lighting.

What an advance for the domestic interior designer to have such flexibility at home. Instead of the clumsy incandescent bulb, ubiquitously shaded in paper or silk, there are downlighters and uplighters to build into the scheme, and an extensive selection of original table lamps for specific tasks. Beamed up – or down – these newly poised and angled lights supply general background and task lighting.

10 Whenever a person moves within an 8-feet (2.5-m) radius of the infrared detector built into the "Sensa" light, it switches itself on. Photocells gauge the level of natural light and automatically adjust light output by 25 to 100 percent in direct response to ambient daylight. A world first for Thorn.

11 The aptly named "Expanded Line Kit" from the brilliant design duo of Perry King and Santiago Miranda for Arteluce. Different halogen heads –"Lucy", "Alma", "Tor" and "Ra"– fit low-voltage ceiling roses. The inventive shapes and prismatic reflectors in this range are matched by detailed accent colour designed to catch the light.

1 Wall-mounted spots are the modern equivalent of the old picture light, which cast a localized beam on a single image. Architect Peter Wilson has chosen a task light shaped like a downlighter to illuminate modern furniture.

2 Tightly controlled beams of low-energy light in Candela's "Micron" range vary from a gentle 20W floodlight to a penetrating 75W spotlight, housed in a system.

Low-voltage systems brought light, quite literally, to the architect's fingertips, since low-voltage light (as its name implies) operates on an electrical supply of 12 volts or less. The German lighting designer Ingo Maurer took advantage of this by hanging a collection of bird-like, low-voltage lights on electrical wires strung across the room like a trapeze. "Adjustable or hanging elements create a jungle of light that dances, glides, tilts, balances and rotates and, above all, provides a clear and precise light by which to work, read or dream," he says about his "YaYa HoHo" system, one of the most popular lights of the 1980s.

Technological advances have affected that most traditional, and popular, of fittings, the table lamp. The new generation of table lamps is made from

5 All in a row—the wall lights from Tebong are shielded by reflector shades on trifid-like angular arms.

3 The adaptable "Shuttle" spotlight by Bruno Gecchelin for iGuzzini (see picture **2**, page 108), shown with a different configuration of casings and reflector accessories.

4 "Futura" from Garcia Garay, designed by J. A. Garcia Garay, is a family of lamps which features two aluminium shades that move through a full 360° to open or shut, as well as to vary the angle of the light.

6

7

6 & 7 Four new spotlights, three of them using dichroic bulbs and a monophase track, are iGuzzini's latest minispots, two of which are pictured here. "Disc", designed by Pasquale Ajello (above left), and "Wing", designed by Bruno Gecchelin (above right), both use low-energy 50W 12V bulbs and the spots can be either fitted to a "Limelight" ceiling track or wall-mounted on curved rods. All fittings have a joint that enables power to be delivered through a 360° vertical and horizontal swing.

8

8 "Poe" from Giugiaro Design, made by Lucitalia, is a low-voltage system for ceilings and walls. Lamps are fully adjustable on support arms and electrical circuits allow full rotation.

9

9 "Contacto" by Belux is a contact plug system for halogen lamps, in which 125 combinations can be created out of 18 elements. The Jurgen Medeback design can be wall-mounted or set on lighting tracks.

Shape Memory Alloy, more commonly used in orthodontics and auto bumpers, since the alloy has a memory that responds to heat. For example, a horseshoe shape cut from the metal and crumpled into a corkscrew, when warmed will return to its original shape. So a lotus petal of a light will, when warmed up as the light burns within a tightly closed bud, gradually unfurl. Other than the visual senses are challenged too; Kreon's inventive lights diffuse scent as the light warms, working on the principle that with dichroic low-voltage systems, the source passes heat backward rather than in the path of light, thus scenting the room.

As lighting technology has become increasingly flexible and responsive, the ability of lights to accentuate is being pushed to new limits by designers. Two

10   12

11

10 "Duo" is a low-voltage lamp designed by Erwin Egli, systemized by Diefo Bally for Belux. Two individual lamp elements, with a 100V transformer fitted to a ceiling strip, form a single unit designed to be suspended over a table. Both lamp elements move up and down on a system of chromium-plated counterweights, and opal and blue glass contribute strongly to its elegant presentation.

11 & 12 Spotlights positioned on beams, rather than attached to the more usual lighting tracks, help to demonstrate the flexibility of a system of spotlighting that here has low-voltage transformers built into neat, cylindrical fittings.

1 The quality of light emitted, the controlled direction of the halogen beam and the splendid formality of this lamp, the "P-1170" by Estiluz, merit the description "classical".

2 "L'Escala" by Estudi Blanc for Metalarte is a metallic floor lamp with an adjustable diffuser and a dimmer control switch on the wiring.

4 The "Bi-Arp" lamp, by Enrico Bona for Skipper Pollux, has a base and stem in transparent plexiglass and a sanded Pyrex glass reflector.

3 "Mantide" by Mauro Canfori for Oluce inclines gracefully on a slender stem, which supports a widened bowl that pools the halogen beam.

5 The overhanging, pendulous floor light that enshrines the lamp source in a large, shaded fitting makes a useful task light in this room by John Pawson, who tries to avoid ceiling lights in his interiors.

6 "Maja" by Sergi Devesa for Metalarte uses indirect halogen light on top of a swivelling support, which is metallized graphite grey and chromium-plated.

Spaniards, Bigas and Sant (see page 28), have produced an aluminium moulding which lights a lamp wherever one is clipped in, and is ideal for stairs or to illuminate pictures. And furniture makers outline features with built-in lights and create backlit panels in storage systems; for example, a bevelled glass edge on a shelf will have a fine line of light running along it. The latest trend is to use metal-halide discharge lamps, which are brighter yet cooler than dichroic low-voltage bulbs.

As designers explore shape, the result is less a light show of dazzling theatricality than a collection of new lights assembled with the express notion that "light can evoke fantasy and fable, create effects and get involved in shadow play", as the organizers of Euroluce, the lighting industry's international lighting fair, claim.

8 "Victory" by De Pas, D'Urbino and Lomazzi is a floor or extendable wall lamp in lacquered metal with a porcelain diffuser to soften the 300W halogen bulb. On a lacquered metal structure, it is made by Stilnovo.

9 Coveted design award Compasso d'Oro has been won on several occasions by designer Rodolpho Bonetto, whose "Eviter" floor light uses a diffuser of pressed, satin-etched glass, made by Luci.

7 "Sinclina" is an inclined lamp by Estudi Blanc for Metalarte. Its height can be adjusted by lowering the light on its anodized silver or black column.

10 Unusually, "Penombra" by Antoni Flores for Gargot uses low-energy fluorescent tubes and a reflector within its slender aluminium body. It is available in either a matte-anodized or a matte-gold finish, and stands on a cast-aluminium base.

16 This free-standing lamp, "Aeto", is by Fabio Lombardo for Flos. It is nearly 6.5 feet (1.96 m) tall and uses a single 450W halogen bulb.

12 Halogen bulbs on free-standing uplighters will throw a strong wash of light up to the ceiling. Uplighters such as this, used by architect David Wild, need to be set above eye level to avoid glare from the bulbs.

13 Free-standing lights can be moved to where the light is most needed. Depending on the shade and reflectors, they can be either up- or downlighters, like the "Berenice" by Luceplan.

14 "Stele" by Jurgen Medeback for Belux offers indirect lighting on a pair of slender columns that are so attenuated they make the piece more sculptural than a mere lamp.

11 A diffused-lighting halogen lamp, "Sake," by Paolo and Marco Piva for Stilnovo, was made as either a floor or wall lamp in anthracite, metallic blue or green. It has a lacquered, aluminium-moulded body and a sand-blasted diffuser.

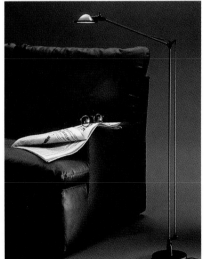

15 Like Santiago Calatrava's architecture, the "Montjuic" for Artemide appears to defy the laws of gravity. The painted-fibre, diagonal support for the tubular halogen lamp neatly conceals the cord.

11   **13**   **14**

16

1 Post-modernist architect Michael Graves designed a series of lamps for Baldinger Architectural Lighting. His "Urbino" lantern, made of brass and white opal acrylic, is an imposing 35 inches (89 cm) high.

3 The "Firenze" wall sconce from Michael Graves, manufactured by Baldinger Architectural Lighting is made of brass and white opal acrylic.

2 Soft polyurethane is used by Fabian for "Gum" 705D07 wall lamp, available with interchangeable colour spots.

8 The "Aramis" by Gourdon and Brux for Luxo has a satinated glass diffuser. It takes a 300W halogen or 70W metal halide bulb (shown here) with column to hold the ignitor and capacitor.

9 "Estiluz" A1133 halogen wall light by Leonardo Marelli. It uses a 220W halogen bar behind a satin glass shade held in a disc that can be black pearlized or gold finished.

4 "Eco" by Giugiaro Design for Luci has a swivelling cone-shaped reflector in stove-enamelled metal. It is available in many colours and holds a single 250W linear-halogen bulb.

5 & 6 Best of Brass stock a wide range of switches that give a conventional frame to a plain, unadorned switch plate. And from Clipsal, sockets, TV and telephone outlets and shaver sockets in impact-resistant polycarbonate.

7 "Bisbi" by Achille Castiglioni is a wall light with a ceramic socket and a die-cast aluminium rotating reflector, from Flos. A twist of the ring changes it from uplighter to wall-washer.

10 "Vulcanos" by Sergi Devesa for Metalarte is a wall bracket that can be fitted to the ceiling. It has a swivelling metal arm and a matte, tempered glass diffuser to shield the low-energy, 15W halogen light bulb.

13

13 Breaking out of the Murano glass mould to create enlightened fittings, Barovier and Toso took the design of Giusto Toso and created a range of floor, wall and ceiling lights called "Flu".

14 A wall-mounted light, the "Evipar" by designer Rodolgo Bonetto, houses a 500W linear halogen bulb in a stove-enamelled support. It is available in a range of different colours, with a diffuser in acid-etched, pressed glass, and is produced by Lucitalia.

14

15

16

15 Stilnovo's "Victory" by de Pas, D'Urbino and Lomazzi is of lacquered metal with a porcelain diffuser. The floor-standing version of this light is shown on page 112 (picture **8**).

17 The "Malibu" follows maestro Ettore Sottsass' enthusiasm for place-naming his designs. His wall light for Stilnovo is in white or anodized aluminium with a lacquered metal body and a glass diffuser that houses a single 60W bulb.

18 "Pleak" designed by Nemo and made by Tebong gracefully supports on a ledge this 200W pencil-slim linear halogen lamp on its epoxyated steel book frame.

11 **18**

16 The horn-shaped light became Philippe Starck's leitmotif in the New York Royalton. Each of the 30-40 doors in that hotel's lobby supports above it a crystal light fixture like the "Lucefair", subsequently put into production by Flos.

20 Ingo Maurer extends his concept of light in motion with the bird-like "Eclipse-elipse", which hovers on the wall on touch-sensitive cords and controls that do away with traditional wiring and switches. The light holds a 50W bulb with a swivelling mirror to reflect and direct light.

17

12

19 A hinged flap like a torch flips the light head back or swivels it on this "Land" wall light, designed by architect Robert Pamio for Leucos. It can also be ceiling-mounted, and is equipped with two movements that rotate the structure on its axis through 360°, and also allows just the head to rotate on a hinge through 90°. This freedom of movement gives either directional control of the beam or a more generalized light effect.

11 Architects Studio Epton had to work with lights bought by their clients. By flooding the room with natural light, these simple spots were sufficient.

12 "Trybeca" by Bernhard Dessecker shields two halogen bulbs. The wall light can move up or down and swivel on its adjustable fixture.

19

20

1 "Torino" ceiling fixtures from the Michael Graves collection by Baldinger Architectural Lighting in brass with white opal octagonal glass.

2 Woka's 1032 "Mini" by Walter Schmögner in brass with metallic green details holds eight 12V halogen spots on spider-like supports.

3 A customized design by Michael Graves for a pendant fixture. It re-creates the American Ranch-type spoked wheel concept and has three candelabraed torch lights.

4 The "Verona" lamp from the Michael Graves collection, by Baldinger, is a recessed ceiling fixture with trim in antique brass holding the white opal, conical-shaped glass shield.

5 World-famous modernist architect Cini Boeri, working with Murano glass, brings craftsmanship to a functional form with "Feltro".

6 "Lucia" is designed by architect Cini Boeri, who manages to blend craft skills, age-old Murano glass and good functional design.

7 "Bergamo" chandelier from the Michael Graves collection for Baldinger, shown in antique brass. Other finishes and customized heights available.

8 "Spilla" designed by Luciano Pasgani for Arteluce is a ceiling light with a 200W halogen bulb, backlit by a pressed and etched-glass diffuser.

9 When the "Atena", by Ezio Didone for Arteluce, is seen from below, a star-burst of light appears in the conical glass diffuser, which is held either by a matte-grey enamelled reflector or by a sanded glass disc coloured opalescent pink, blue, white or green.

10 "Nebula" by Jordi Vilardell for Gargot houses a 500W halogen lamp in a matte, metallic-grey disc.

11 Thomas Edison's incandescent light is here invoked by Valerio Sacchetti for Sirrah in a lamp holder entitled "Edison 45".

12 Lovegrove and Brown designed the "Bab-ilis" metal ceiling light for Metalarte. Its pressed-glass diffuser shields a 100W bulb.

13 & 14 Pendants that are adjustable make useful work-surface or dining-table illuminations. The "Gavina" (see in detail below right) by Josep Llusca for Blauet is extendable, with a chromium-plated stick to adjust the height of two crystal lampshades shielding either 50W or 75W halogen lamps.

15 Michael Graves' selfconscious emulation of floral forms reverts to Art Nouveau, but the geometry of this pendulous pendant is post-modernist rather than organic.

16 "Futura", designed by J. A. Garcia Garay, is equipped with two aluminium shades that open and shut, and revolve 360° around the 500W bulb.

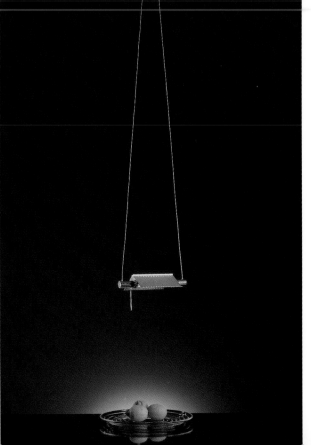

LIGHTING

1 & 2 Murano glass from Venice has been collected for centuries, and Foscarini pride themselves on focusing on functionality as well as aesthetics with their range of lights, "Colora", designed by Vecchiato and Ricci.

4 "Vaticana", designed by Josep Llusca for Metalarte, is a metallic portable table lamp. It has a dimmer switch incorporated into its base and a Pergacel winged shade set into the graphite-grey cone.

3 "Calder" is a halogen lamp designed by Enric Ranch for Metalarte as a desk light with dimmer switch. It stands nearly 16 inches (40 cm) high, with a reach of 36 inches (92.5 cm).

10 The "Pap" floor lamp is a faithful copy of the original, designed in 1923 by Gyula Pap. Plate glass is connected by a nickel-plated tubular unit to a black-lacquered iron baseplate.

5 If it were necessary to define an elementary solution for task lighting, it would probably be similar to this small table light, "Bluebird", by Jorge Pensi for Belux.

7 A sober, matte-black design from Samuel Ribet called "Heron", for Stilnovo, houses a 50W 12V halogen bulb in lacquered metal. The lighting arm is adjustable.

6 A thin, rod-like support holds a dichroic halogen bulb and reflector in Shiro Kuramata's original lamp called "Hydrogen Dream". The light was designed in 1988.

9 Like a "Metronome" in name and characteristics, J. Garcia Garay's table lamp moves side to side for use as a reading lamp, while from inside the sand-blasted crystal shade, a gentle light permeates the room.

11 F. Fabbian and F. lli created a series of metal-and-glass lights, designed by G.P. Derai, called "Master", "Major", "Big" and, shown here, "Senior". There is also a scaled-down "Junior".

8 From designer Sergi Devesa for Metalarte comes "Zen". This brushed-aluminium table light stands 6.5 inches (16.5 cm) high and will accommodate a single bulb up to a maximum output of 25W.

12 & 13 In a conversion of a 19th-century terrace house, Jan Kaplicky of Future Systems placed banks of switches in the aluminium sheets that line the false floor, beneath which pipes and cables run.

13

14 Philippe Starck's unusual adjustable table lamp, "ARA" for Flos, is turned on and off by grasping the horn-shaped shade. The lamp is chromium-plated cast aluminium.

12

14

17 Woka Lamps' chain-styled desk light, designed by Udo Maurer, certainly has a presence, and perhaps even an air of menace.

17

18 Designed by Ferdinand Porsche and Christian Schwamkrug for PAF, "Jazz" folds flat like a handset. When in operation, its two-stage, telescopic arm allows a variety of lighting positions. A dimmer switch is incorporated.

15 Woka "159" is from a collection designed by Josef Hoffmann and Adolf Loos. This classic series of lamps draws on the past for its inspiration, this one being originally designed in 1925.

16 Mario Barbaglia and Marco Colombo designed the poised "Dove" for PAF. It is an adjustable halogen lamp, with tubular supports in polished black. The base and lighting arm are in matte-black, white, yellow, red or blue.

15

16

18

LIGHTING

1 A table lamp leaning forward to cast light upon the page at the required angle is Asahara Sigeaki's "Tokio" for Stilnovo – a 500W 12V halogen light with an adjustable inclination of lacquered metal, and the mekralon reflector holding a built-in transformer.

2 "Lola" by C. Bermudo for Marset stands 22 inches (55cm) high on a crescent-shaped base.

3 "Tizio" by Richard Sapper for Artemide marked in the 1970s the first of the new generation of low-voltage lights. Set on a swivelling piece of scaffolding, the light has become a design icon on contemporary worktops.

4 "Tolomeo", by Michele de Lucchi and Giancarlo Fassina, stands in Gary Cunningham's conversion of an electricity sub-station conversion. The lamp shows the tension wires that allow the arms to move at a touch.

8 Lampshade makers traditionally use parchment paper, a material seldom seen in modern lighting where glass or metal diffuse the beam. But for Woka's Art Collection, Jörg Wurmitzer revived "pergament" paper as a reflector for three halogen spots on a brass-and-wood fixture.

5 "Zoom" lives up to its name by elongating its probe-like head, or zigzagging up on its rods out of the way. Patrick Magnin for Arteluce uses either one or two 50W halogen bulbs with rotating reflectors.

6 Inventive creator of "One From the Heart", Ingo Maurer, describes this light as an adjustable bedside lamp, its romantic form made of metal, glass and plastic. It stands 37 inches (95 cm) high.

7 "Hasard" by Ingo Maurer is intentionally industrial with a raw, hand-made base and shade. The light turns, bends, swivels, and stretches to a height of nearly 18 inches (45 cm) and has a 50W halogen bulb.

Storage

2

Previous page
Banks of beech drawers and cupboards, equipped with simple metal D-handles, provide bedroom storage in a house by David Chipperfield.

1 Frosted glass supports for clear Crown glass shelves with their bevelled green edges on aluminium tubes are Andreas Weber's storage solution in an 18th-century apartment.

Storage, that boring hold-all, hide-all for so many things that each and every one of us needs to give long-term house room to, is one of the most fickle aspects of modern living. Essentials that had to be stored a century ago would reveal a different lifestyle, different preoccupations – even different uses of leisure time – from those with which we are familiar with today. The products – and their proportions – have changed for a start. The music room no longer houses a piano and wind-up gramophone with its pile of fragile, 78 rpm records. Instead there are the compact disc player and speakers. Even the study or home office, which replaces the library, is now dominated by the computer, monitor, printer and fax and telephone back-up, all housed in their own lightweight, mobile storage systems. How to accommodate the changing technology at the same time as living companionably with your possessions easily at hand is the crux of modern storage.

A decade ago, storage walls of shelves

122

2 A wall-mounted ziggurat by Duravit offers 18 drawers of varying size for the accumulated trivia of everyday life while freeing valuable floor space in a small room for other use.

3 Made of pear, amaranth and rosewood, Driade's "Eloise" by Antonia Astori is beautifully crafted.

4 Interlubke recognize the need for open shelving in "Duo-tone". Linked with the matching "Cockpit" desk, it provides easy access to everything from music to tax returns.

3

5 Architect John Pawson demonstrates his belief that space is the most luxurious thing a minimalist can provide. Enormous storage blocks, capable of holding a vast amount of material out of sight, rid the room of unnecessary objects and clutter.

4

and cupboards stacked on top of each other seemed to be the answer. They were even known as working walls. Today, the lack of floor space that results from expensively engineered systems of stacking shelves makes these systems obsolete. Extendable trolleys, lightweight wall runners capable of supporting long spans of shelves, work units with vertebral cord systems to hide the tangle of wires behind every work-efficient electronic system, and sculptural wardrobe accessories such as coatstands and the valet to hold shoes, slacks and ties, all free-standing, represent modern attempts to balance aesthetics with practicality.

Not everything these days is designed to be small. Weary of the black-box gadgetry that houses electronic equipment from hi-fi to computers, the new designs for sound systems shape them like giant cellos or tubas. Free-standing, they don't require shelving systems to support them.

For most people, the greatest number of items to be stored is in the bedroom, which is usually dominated by fixtures

6 with sliding doors and/or walk-in

5

6 Giant wheels give a fantastic impression of some futuristic, sci-fi airlock system, mounted on four huge sliding units, designed by architect John Young. Inside the steel-panelled units are easy-access

corridors giving onto space sufficient to house acres of domestic clutter.

7

7 Tebong gives an intriguing interpretation to the umbrellas housed in this stand, inverted so that its spokes replicate the shapes of the furled umbrellas within.

1 Using a base of ball bearings held between two discs of glass, the Tonelli "Cactus" is a free-standing angular bookshelf. A single sheet of clear glass provides support for the V-shaped shelves.

2 Like the "Cactus", Tonelli's "Albero" provides six angular shelves, holding books at 45°. Also resting on a ball-bearing base, the structure of sheet glass creates a zigzag pattern – a geometric extension of "Cactus".

3 Marcello Morandini's imaginative manipulation of geometry, in his free-standing "Corner" shelving for Rosenthal Furniture, is made of five differently sized components to provide a flexible storage unit.

4 The black uniformity with coloured edgings of "Corner" (see 3) makes it both similar and complementary to "Mobile", also by Marcello Morandini for Rosenthal.

5 Pruning back the bulk and paring down describe architect Eva Jiricna's free-hanging shelving design. Thick sheet glass rests on small stoppers attached to thin steel wires hanging from a girder-like support bolted securely to the wall. Maximum storage space is provided without blocking any sight lines.

6

7

8

6, 7, 8 Archille Castiglioni's "Joy" table for Zanotta extends from two horizontal platforms into seven, pivoting from a central column, like a flight of stairs, or acts as a multi-level storage unit.
9 Before the 1980s, glass could not be cut into the exacting shapes demanded by modern storage systems. Then the laser cutter arrived, allowing safety glass to be cut into the shapes seen here, in "Scenario" by Tonelli.

cupboards. In the contemporary apartment, some rooms can be so small that it becomes simpler by far to hang clothes on the types of open rails favoured by shop and store fitters, thereby converting a single bedroom to a storage system. Unconventional storage solutions come from designers who use fitters' furniture, from fashion store swing rails to garage mechanics' toolbox trolleys. Extendable arms used with hospital beds have been redeployed as domestic bedside tables so that the television, telephone or books can be readily brought to hand. In a child's room, the bed is often elevated above the cupboard space, with a ladder ascent and an enclosing safety rail. "Honey, I Shrunk the Kids" is the title of a popular movie of the late 1980s, and while the advantages of making people Lilliputian are obvious, the reality is that more and more people are occupying smaller and smaller living spaces. In every case, the answer to storage is to draw up a list of your priorities. There is no one answer because everybody's list will differ. Modern systems usually give you somewhere to store the single fold-up bed when it is not required by sliding it into a recess. Such features as corner

9

10 The all-glass, wall-mounted library from Marais, the "MB 1500", is made of five half-moon-shaped glass shelves within a transparent frame.
11 This system of fixed shelving was designed by Munkenbeck & Marshall. The custom-built storage is tall and deep enough for more than just books. Frosted glass wrapped around cylindrical wall fittings provides stable, but non-adjustable, shelving.

10

11

12

12 Fucina, part of the Skipper group, manufactured the "Cidonio" bookshelf in scogliera grey marble, designed by Afra and Tobia Scarpa.

125

1 Landing-pad feet connect the new Enea "Naos" aluminium storage unit, designed by Gabriel Teixidó, to its shelves, which can be fixed to the ceiling, wall or floor.

2 & 3 Designed for Driade's modular "Oikos" system by Antonia Astori, "Cubo" (above left) consists of modules, each containing six boxes. In the same system is the slimline "Favo" for the small room (above right).

4 The three-tiered bridge of the versatile "Naos" system is by Teixidó.

5 Tecta's "S 69" system consists of five curvaceous black and blue panels connected by three coloured boxes and a drawer.

6 These metal storage frames, as roundly folded as fabric yet firm in their support, were designed by architect Eva Jiricna.

carousels or lazy susan racks, stacking shoe racks, containers for storing clothes, and suitcases, in the hard-to-get-at upper parts, are revealed behind space-saving sliding doors. Built-in lighting is also usually a feature.

Fashionable hanging systems are revealed in the bedroom with the new sculptural furniture designed to hold clothing draped over it. Lord Snowdon's design now in production, entitled "Weekend Wardrobe", looks like a wooden ladder, the top rung supporting a slanted mirror, and each of the other rungs holding trousers and ties. Two broad leather straps are provided to support shallow pouches large enough for several shirts and, at the base, shoes. De Pas, d'Urbino and Lomazzi designed for the Italian company Zanotta a teepee of clustered sticks, each one notched to hold an article of clothing; a

7 This central storage facility by architect Franklin D. Israel usefully combines an artwork display area on one side and adjustable shelving for records or a hi-fi system on the other.

8 The blue central column of Interlubke's ziggurat consists of two cupboards and four drawers, flanked on the left by two glass cabinets and, on the right, by five open shelves for easy access to often used objects, such as the stereo.

telescopic tensile-steel arc from Spanish Disform adjusts to bow beneath ceiling and floor, with adjustable knobs sliding up and down the bowed rods to hold whatever is required; even the low-cost retail furnishing group from Sweden, Ikea, sells in its worldwide outlets sculptural male and female wire outlines, life-sized, for you to cover up with clothing.

These sculptural forms are a mobile though less-substantial alternative to furniture lined up against the walls, which tends to become part of the fabric of the house. Bedrooms in modern houses are rarely larger than about 12 feet by 10 feet (3.5 metres by 3 metres), which means that floor space is limited to just one wall dedicated to built-in cupboards, or else the individual pieces that literally come out of the closet. A free-standing chest of drawers

9 Architect Eva Jiricna designed these thick glass shelves on metal cylinders to provide spacious wall-to-wall storage. The television is supported on a pivoting metal bracket.
10 Wire mesh, spiky feet and a small flag give this bookcase by J. Borris a medieval look.
11 The five shelves and the frame of the Marais "Mec 500" system simply rest

casually unsupported against the wall.
12 Enea's wall-to-wall design has open shelves that are fixed to extruded aluminium clamps by non-skid polythene discs. These clamps are attached to side channels within the metal stanchions so that shelves can be fixed at any height.

1 A home library of books can be housed in this capacious shelving unit from Interlubke. It contains 32 storage boxes and six drawers on the central column of five.

2 Interlubke's long closet system provides a "working wall" for clothes storage. This modular system with hinged doors is both smart and practical, shown here in a combination of cupboards and drawers in both natural wood and white lacquer.

8 Architect David Wild has gained valuable additional storage areas in his own house by using normally inaccessible staircase space, with panelled wood cupboards and shelves reachable from the stairs above by stretching out over the railing.

3, 4 & 5 Interlubke's highly versatile freestanding TV/video bar, "Duo-center", designed by Siegried Bensinger, rotates through 360° on its central pole. Its design makes it suitable for private living space, but it could be successfully used in an office as well. Other views of the "Duo-center" reveal perforated mesh back panels to ventilate the TV compartment, and a drawer beneath the VCR shelf for storing tapes.

6 Marshall Erdman's frameless "Techline" closet system is predrilled to receive a variety of hinges, glides or shelf supports. Its laminated case is surrounded by PVC, eased to a soft radius.

7 Built around a doorway, Arc Linea's "Odeon" by designer Carlo Bartoli, permits easy access from both sides of the wall. It is available in black- or white-lacquered Italian walnut.

takes up less overall space but requires more free space in front of it so that you can pull out the drawers. The façade of each built-in bedroom depends on cupboard doors, and such a line-up determines the style of the room — hence the contemporary fashion for paint finishes on cheap wood veneers.

Storage needs vary within each household. A professional designer will ask his or her client a range of questions in order to determine the best storage configuration. For example, a kitchen planner will ask the following: How many meals do you prepare a day? What sort of food do you like? How much cooking equipment do you use? How many sets of dishes do you own? Do you eat in a separate dining room with its own storage facilities? The professional person living alone who owns a microwave and small freezer box probably needs very

9 The cupboards in this house, designed by architects Gwathmey Siegel cleverly follow the contours of this unusual room to form a barrier between the living area and the glass-encased hollow shaft onto the floor above. Logs for the fire are stored in the single-piece concrete box at the end of the unit.

10 This unit is a custom-built design by David Chipperfield. Eight cherrywood drawers of increasing size run the length of the unit. Recessed in the unit, a TV is on a sliding drawer. Two high cupboards provide additional storage for material not often needed.

little space for canned or dried goods and just a window box for herbs. The large family kitchen with a gas-fired range and a walk-in pantry clearly needs storage space for heavyweight cast-iron cooking pots, a dishwasher, dishes, and space for basic foodstuffs bought in bulk. Glasses, utensils and china all need storage space, sensibly hidden behind cupboard doors or on open display.

Ease of access, with the heavier objects on a lower level and objects in constant use in front, encourages professional cooks to hang their utensils and other equipment on open hooks above the work-tops or counters. Versatile, ventilated pantry cupboards and smaller cup-boards with wire baskets for vegetables, bread or pastries are also available. Storage in the main living area is more exacting, less specific. Here, friends are entertained, television is watched, the VCR is housed and music is listened to.

1 This configuration of the Arc Linea "Odeon" by designer Carlo Bartoli creates a doorway out of closed cupboards. The variety of drawers, cupboards and boxes means that normally wasted space can be brought into play. For other "Odeon" variations see pages 128 and 133.

2 Tadao Ando's house is of the typically minimalist Japanese style, using basic drawers made of simple wood. These rest against a stone pillar, which also provides an end to the counter on which the bowls rest.
3 The curvaceous desk hugs the rounded wall in this Le Corbusier house, La Villa Turque. Andrée Putman designed the interior to wrap around the house like a second skin.

4 Driade's "Oikos" system takes on a new dimension by using metal in its "Dilemma" storage system. The reflective qualities of the material give the room a feeling of greater space and depth.

5 Two wooden cupboards without handles are positioned under the Gaggenau oven on this storage unit, made entirely of pine, by David Chipperfield. Spartan designs like this make suitable storage for any room in the house.

6 Architect John Pawson displays here the monastic principles that underlie his designs.

7 Thin panels have been arranged into a gently sinuous storage unit in architect Franklin D. Israel's design. Without doors or hidden shelving, three glass shelves jut out from the far end of the wall, and below these is a simple square fireplace with a flat polished hearth in front of it.

6

5

8

8 Driade's system by Antonia Astori is an unusual departure in this "Abaco" configuration. The combination of glass, laminate and tubular metal is a colourful accompaniment to the "Oikos" system.

9

9 Interlubke's solution to retrieving items from high-level storage is a rail built just below the topmost shelf of this seven-layer wooden unit. A simple metal ladder can then easily be attached between the rail and the floor, providing easy access to the higher shelves, without the need for a bulky step ladder or for resting an ordinary ladder on the shelving itself.

7

1 Roll-up doors slide back into the cabinet to reveal the contents of these multi-purpose "Perseo" storage units by Estudi Blanc.

5 Piero Fornasetti, who died in 1988, left behind a legacy of brilliant design work and architectural perspectives, a tradition carried on by his son, Barnaba, in pieces such as his classic screens and this commode.

2 Artespana focus on the VCR storage problem with "Maya", a trapezoid shelving system looking like truncated pyramids, designed by P.G. Bellas.

3 Modular units looking like clones need distinctive colouring and detailing, such as these inverted triangular and dot metallic handles, to make their simple form, adaptable to any space, stand out. "Cubiform" is designed by Estudi Blanc.

4 Built on the bean-stalk principle, this storage system by Pepe Bonet for Bd Ediciones de Diseno offers a visionary approach to the problem of limited floor space.

6 Designer Jeannot Cerutti's totemistic unit, "Libabel", for Sawaya & Moroni has tensile wires to hold the contents in place.

This space also has to double as a library and a display area for objects. Wall space must be freed for shelves at the right height both for viewing and for access. Specific siting next to power outlets as well as cable lengths determine the positioning of electronic equipment, surrounded by clear floor space for furniture so that the entertainment they offer can be enjoyed.

Worse, wall space will be at a premium – every radiator panel, window, large-scale piece of furniture limits your storage options. Purpose-built storage systems are sometimes free-standing and ideally suited to deal with this problem by creating a room divider. A line-up of shelves on adjustable tracks against the wall is another solution, one that also provides extra insulation and soundproofing – no insulation material is as thick as a covering of paperbacks.

8 From Rosenthal comes "Life Service" by Jochen Flack – a mobile sideboard that brings cutlery, plates, glasses to the table. Its flap extensions provide instant work surfaces and pivoting drawers give easy access.

9 This combination filing cabinet and desk employs cleverly angled geometry in a thoughtful storage solution. Still in prototype, it is by architect Klaus Block, whose interesting work, exhibited by avante-garde furniture movement Berliner Zimmer, has attracted attention at many furniture fairs. Berliner Zimmer claim to kick out against the "upright worthiness" of much of German design.

7 Arc Linea's "Odeon" is an impressive wall shelving system, constructed from Italian walnut, with a high-gloss, black- or white-lacquered finish. It is designed by Carlo Bartoli and it combines in one unit both open and closed display space, depending on what is required.

10 "Kuubi", by Pirkko Stenros for Muurame, is a modular series which had items added to it each year, so that over the 1980s it grew from a simple collection to an all-purpose storage system for any room in the home.

11, 12, 13, 14 & 15 Cult movie of the 1980s, "Batman", featured crafted cabinetry by Jamie Tresserra Clapes. With high standards of craftsmanship, and only 25 pieces made of each design, his small collection of furniture is highly prized. These different views show his hand-made walnut "Samuro" unit, which, like its Japanese namesake, is guardian of all the family's possessions.

16 The inverted triangular sides of the free-standing "Laurenziana" unit, which is designed by Colantoni, Contini and Stella, provide an improbable balancing act for a series of clear glass shelves.

STORAGE

1 This "Taka" coatstand in black enamelled metal with a black marquina marble base is from Atrium.

2 An anorexic coat rack, "N.A.U.", from Inno, runs like a seamstress' thread up the wall to end in a convenient, four-fingered hook.

3 The ubiquitous metal clothes rail, so favoured by dress manufacturers for storage and delivery, is here interpreted in a very individual way by the design company Tebong. The result is a stylish and sturdy yet inexpensive little free-standing wardrobe.

4 Designed by Salvadó and Solé, this haloed hatstand is called "Percha". The user will find that, like its name, this little detail is the easiest and tidiest way to accommodate a winter overcoat, a scarf and a hat on one single clamp attached to the wall.

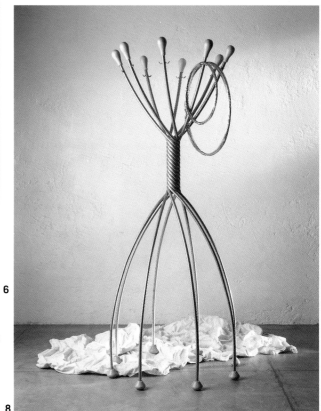

5 The purpose of "Magazine", a flapped rack designed by Piero de Longhi for Atrium, speaks for itself.

6 This interestingly frazzled silhouette called "Parrucca" for Disform, by the trio De Pas, D'Urbino and Lomazzi, offers you many angles on which to hang your hat and coat.

7 Fashionable hang-ups are revealed by Carl F. Petersen's utensil rod. Butcher's hooks are supposed to be a useful storage adjunct, until you try to find them that is. No such problems here!

8 The aptly named "Octopus" wraps around its slender stem to branch out into an imposing steel structure, by Zero Disengo.

Bathrooms

Previous page

Previous page
Architect John Young
installed S-shaped
tubular chrome bars to
warm towels and
compliment a stainless
steel basin and an
Eileen Gray mirror.
1 From the former
team of Pawson and
Silvestrin comes this
minimalist design.
A chink of light filtered
through a triangular
wall highlights the
travertine basin and its
curved tap. A slabbed
Santanyi stone floor
and matte-white walls
reinforce a monastic
approach to bathing.
2 An old power
substation, converted
by architect Gary
Cunningham, has
many surfaces in the
raw, reflecting the
building's utilitarian
heritage.

The best contemporary bathrooms are those that cloak
fitness for purpose in a
Spartan simplicity, thus
conforming with Western
cultural traditions based on
ideas of segregation and
minimum contact. In the 1990s, despite
what appears to be people's preoccupation with health and body consciousness,
few have turned over one of the larger
rooms in the home to a health spa with
whirlpool bathtub or sauna. Health-
conscious exercise devotees have,
however, pioneered some new uses for
the bathroom, turning it into a mini-gym
by installing such items as an exercise
rail against a mirrored wall, as well as
the new compact rowing or treadmill
walking machines that are designed
to be folded flat against the wall when
not in use.

It is a sobering reflection that there
have been so few innovations since the
Romans introduced hot, piped water
into soak tubs, still visible today in
the old spa towns. In America in 1931,
Buckminster Fuller introduced his as-
tonishing Dymaxion bathroom, a mobile

3 A post-modernist
Gothic spirit can be
discerned in this oval-
shaped basin, entitled
"Point", produced
by Dornbracht,
which is housed in a
hexagonal top and
supported on a
triangular lectern base.

1

2

5

6 The open plumbing on a stainless steel washbasin, set against a midnight-blue bath panel, emphasizes the high-tech approach of the architects of this bathroom. They designed contrasts and repeats in the many reflective surfaces used in the scheme.

6

3

4

4 Stone is the favourite hard surface for bathrooms, since it is waterproof and easy to clean. A trio of accessories from Dornbracht on a slab of granite echo that material's same hard-edged and geometric form.

5 This bathroom in a riverside apartment was designed by architect John Young. The girdle of tubular stainless steel carries both the plumbing and heating pipes. This same circular form is replicated in the

shower rail above, while the bath is a cedarwood Japanese tub, sealed for safety reasons when not in use. Pilkington's double-glazed roof panels keep this penthouse room light and warm.

7

7 "The best hotels are always unpretentious, abstractly comfortable, never challenging," says Andrée Putman, whose hotel-designed bathroom products are now available for the domestic market from Societe André.

137

room cast as a single sculptural unit of pressed steel and inserted into his Dymaxion prefab house. But his patented idea for the American Radiator Company never really caught on, possibly since bathroom detailing is too cumbersome to transport easily.

Fitted as it is to the wall with pipework inlets and outlets, the contemporary bathroom is the most inflexible room in the home to plan. Since it is also the most dedicatedly equipped room, with fittings and fixtures that have only a single function, it is the most difficult space to utilize for another purpose. Furthermore, planning regulations concerning the plumbing of waste pipes and water sources vary from country to country. For example, in the United States it is permissible to have a bathroom leading directly off a bedroom, while in Italy there has to be a lobby space between the two rooms.

All these factors make bathroom planning no easy task. While sales networks provide kitchen buyers with a complete service, from design to installation and redecoration, bathroom suppliers tend to provide only a basic service of plumbing and installation. Unlike kitchen design, bathroom design is

1 This California bathroom, designed by architect Arata Isozaki, secluded and meditative within white walls, is finely fitted with banks of storage units, like kitchen cabinets. The window visible here is in fact one of three set high in the south wall, leaving plenty of unbroken wall space lower down.

2 Mass-produced modular units provide ample storage behind the doors that hide the plumbing, and also support the basin. Marble-effect "Clip-stone" vinyl flooring from Amtico replicates real stone.

3 In this bathroom, by architects Gwathmey Siegel, modular units make use of a narrow space. Oval basins, symmetrically placed either side of the tub, incorporate modern comfort into a classical theme.

4

5

4 & 5 A recessed bathtub sunk into a raised platformed area will give the illusion of an increase in the height of a room, especially a small one. This is particularly the case in a bathroom such as this, which is also fitted with mirrored walls. The designer, architect Michael Carapettan, has concealed the controls for the hydromassage tubs beneath the sculptured form of the 5-mm thick moulded fibreglass metacrylic material.

6

6 Designer Finn Skoedt at Studio Rapsel produced "Euclide", this sculptural column washbasin made of chrome-plated metal.

8

9

7 Milldue's vanity units and counters in walnut, laminate or polyester veneers have matching tops in granite. Their "Clio" collection supports an oval basin on an overhanging worksurface, freeing valuable floor space.

7

8 The cabinet, which incorporates an illuminated mirror, is in the "Giamo" range from Duravit. It liberates the room from line-ups of built-in furniture, and its curved lines echo the shapes of the fittings, also by Duravit.

9 Travertine flooring on the curved stairs leading to this bathroom is channelled to allow water to drain away. Design is by architect Peter Wilson in collaboration with architect Chassay Wright.

1 Bathtubs with showers double up on space but need a watertight enclosure when used with a pressure pump. Factory-assembled doors from Daryl include this hinged bath screen, style "950", shown here with white-finish frames and safety glass.

2 In this Majorcan house, designed by the former architectural partnership of Claudio Silvestrin and John Pawson, the austere, yet soaking-sized bathtub is separated from the washbasin by a travertine wall hand-carved from local Santanyi stone.

3 Steps leading to a raised, travertine-tiled area around this tub create the impression of a sunken bath. Architects Gwathmey Siegel offer a leafy view of water, with a louvred blind for privacy. The boxed-in feeling that bathtubs often create is lifted by the tiling, mirrors and glass – and this attractive view.

largely a matter of choosing fittings from builders' suppliers and then piecing together the accessories that will complete the look and co-ordinate with the bathtub, shower and so on. Manufacturers of sanitary fittings and accessories still do not provide overall concept planning for the bathroom.

In the United States, French designers Andrée Putman and Philippe Starck have marketed for the home owner their original designs for hotel bathrooms, found installed in Putman's Morgan's Hotel and Starck's Royalton. This was in response to the lack of

4 A panelled bathtub is lit by a grid of glass blocks, which allow the light that falls at the head to be doubled and returned by the mirrored surfaces. White-on-white detailing gives this city bathroom, designed by architects Gwathmey Siegel, the fresh feeling of a health spa.

4

5

5 Although the wall-mounted telephone in this Trump Tower bathroom in New York, designed by architects Gwathmey Siegel, makes it a contender for a set in Tom Wolfe's "*Bonfire of the Vanities*", the Wall Street effect is somewhat moderated by the use of wood, glass and clay tiles. This imparts an atmosphere of quiet spaciousness to a small room in a city where space is at a premium.

good-looking basin hardware with the backup of matching accessories in the same chrome or lacquer detailing. It is the first step toward the design of the complete bathroom.

Architects are much preoccupied with the troubling issue of the incompatibility of hardware with plumbing fixtures, cupboards and accessories that must be contained within the small area of a bathroom. Research into the amount of space the average adult needs in the bathroom, the room with most equipment and the least space, shows that the minimum clear floor area in front of the bathtub for drying is 43 by 28 inches (100 by 70 cm) and that a space 31 by 24 inches (80 by 60 cm) is needed in front of the lavatory.

Those interested in saving space invariably suggest a shower cubicle to cut down on bathing space. In Japan, however, bathers wash and soap themselves in a space no wider than a narrow corridor, rinse clean and then soak in deep hot tubs that take up little more floor area than the standard shower. The standard Western bathtub measuring 66 inches (167 cm) in length

6 Laufen with Porsche Design reduce conventional bathroom ceramic ware to an oval and triangle, fusing that geometry into a complete, ergonomically designed furnishing system.

6

1

2

1 A high-sided bathtub shaped from a marble block by architect John Pawson features marble grain that runs on the diagonal one way on the bathtub panels, and contrasts with the angle created by the diagonal grain along the floor.

3

2 The "Unica" corner tub in moulded acrylic by Gruppo Novellini offers whirlpool hydrojets.
3 Architect Jan Kaplicky omitted the panels of this Ideal Standard "Michelangelo" bathtub, and set it on the conventional skeletal frame. The toilet and basin are from the same series, all designed by John Beauchamp.

4

5

is now rivalled by the higher-sided, more upright 54-inch (137-cm) bathtub. And the earlier bathtubs made of cast iron, which weighed so much when filled with water, have been replaced by modern versions made of fibreglass and steel, coated in scratch-free coloured finishes. Bathtubs moulded around the human form, with handgrips for leverage, can push the water level up above the parts that longer, more conventional baths cannot reach, though they do tend to look a little coffin-like when seen from above.

Whirlpool baths, with controls to vary the intensity of the jet of water, are a much-lauded, recent domestic introduction. As well, electric pumps that vary the amount of the water flow make it possible to achieve aerated water in the shower. Pumps can also take water

4 Eva Jiricna combines customized steel fittings with manufactured white ceramic ware and a sloping reflective bath panel that effectively reduces the visual volume of this large item.

5 This sinuously designed bathtub, "Sinuosa" by Gruppo Novellini, has three hydrojet massage nozzles, adjustable in intensity and direction, activated by a motor pump.

6 Designer Philippe Starck was commissioned to tackle the old-fashioned Royalton Hotel in New York, formerly a sleazy, turn-of-the-century establishment that had dime-slot waterbeds. Here, in the hotel's Edwardian bathrooms, he brilliantly combines bathtub and shower by creating a semi-circular wall, with a protective circular shower rail.

7 Architects John Pawson's and Claudio Silvestrin's use of a roll-top tub against a minimalist background of a monolithic shower wall exaggerates the scale from the floor up. This is accentuated by the use of giant slabs on the floor and smaller ones on the panel.

7

6

3 Showers are often the last item to be chosen, and so have to respond to the style already set. This shower tray from Cesana's "Boglass" series has a built-in corner seat, and glass panels shaped to follow the tray contours with either pivoting or bi-fold doors.

directly from the main supply and then heat it using a small electric or gas heater fitted close to the shower unit. Water temperature is varied by increasing or decreasing pressure—the higher the flow, the cooler the temperature. The shower market is divided into electric, mixer and power showers and bath/shower mixers. The cheapest to install are simple electric showers, but power showers are the most popular multifunctional models, with heads for spray patterns and a pump to drive the system under pressure.

Basic washbasins can be fixed on a pedestal or wall-hung, usually mounted at a height of 32 inches (81 cm) from floor to rim. The appropriately named "vanity" sets a pair of basins side by side in the manner of the modern deluxe hotel. This is not as bland a mix as it might sound, since this can be the way to line up fittings and bring additional water points into the bathroom without taking up as much space as, for example, two discrete pedestal versions. The shapes of basins are oval, rectangular, square or circular. At Starck's imaginative Café Costes in

4 Along with traditional shower bases and stalls, manufacturers have introduced new, space-utilizing, corner-mounted models, such as the Cesana Sene 700 "Compass".

5 This triangular shower, style "635 Pentagon", by Daryl, fits seamlessly into a 36 x 36-inch (90 x 90-cm) corner. Its pivot-hung door has 8-mm-thick glazing, amply robust to repel the steam generated by the new generation of power showers.

1 For a high-tech apartment, architect Eva Jiricna specified a circular shower, with the heating elements and controls enclosed within this space capsule.

2 With this model, Cesana's "Logic", for the first time the plumbing is marshalled in a pillar alongside the activating mixer valve. In addition, the pillar is also equipped with eight different massage functions.

144

6 Bathroom fittings from Laufen relate to each other in harmonious shapes. The toilet, which has a detachable seat for easy cleaning, is condensation-proofed along the cistern. This is an important consideration when placing fittings in the same room as a shower cubicle.

7 Fitted like a conventionally hinged door that opens outward, the glazed panels either side of this Daryl shower, style "961", open up the entire length of the rectangular stall to give easy and safe access. Glass can be clear, as here, or etched with a grid pattern.

8 A generously sized, chrome-plated shower nozzle is illuminated from above by a circular glass panel set into the bathroom ceiling. The shower head pumps aerated water onto the bather in this fully tiled installation by architect Arata Isozaki.

Paris, triangular glass basins are washed by a water jet from a curvaceous tube above the angled glass, triggered by a floor pedal.

"Warm furnishing" is the marketing catchphrase for the obvious solution to the problem of cold surfaces, exemplified by heated towel bars and underfloor heating that blows warm air out into the room through grills, and the large steel radiators with warm water transmitting heat with rigorous, functional simplicity.

Since bathrooms seldom have vast areas of unshielded windows, natural light often has to be supplemented with artificial illumination. The accurate placing is important – overhead light

9 The Daryl "933" triple-panel sliding door fits any size of shower tray. Ideal in tight spaces, the doors can move left or right behind each other, sliding on a slimline, self-cleaning, grooved track system.

1 Architect John Pawson's inspiration is clear in this bathroom. A slab of marble, angled to fill a shallow channel with water from an overhead spout, takes both its form and function from the old dairies before the time of refrigeration, when channelled marble sinks were vital to the preservation of milk products. Industrial forms are an important influence on Pawson, along with the design traditions of Japan.

1

2

3

4 Duravit, more than 170 years old, specialize in ceramics. Their interchangeable pedestal basins, in the form of a steel cylinder, an urn, a chimney flue and a bronzed fruitwood slab, serve to hide the plumbing.

4

5 Duravit's "Dellarco" white ceramic double basin is state of the art for shared living. Within a small worktop area there are two basins – ideal for working city couples who are short on both space and time.

5

2 The "Pump" washbasin by Agape is made of steel and has tubular supports on either side designed to hold towels – a useful device in a small bathroom.

3 This circular pedestal washbasin, by architect John Pawson, is scooped from a block of marble. Its simplicity and purity of line is accentuated by the tap – a chrome tube that would normally qualify as plumbing and be hidden from sight by the plinth.

and mirrors can create unflattering shadows. Most bathroom lights are low voltage, perhaps arranged on a strip panel above the mirror, or bulkhead lights covered in nonreflective glass, such as those found on board ships. The most successful bathrooms are those that overcome their solemn and frequently unprepossessing functionality with a simplicity of sculptural form and an unostentatious background. Such rooms feature the comfort of hot running water, a fast-jetting shower, capacious basins, warm towels and clean, elegant finishes.

6 Architect Philippe Starck designed his "Lola Hertzburg" stainless steel and chrome basin for Rapsel to be self-sufficient, like the sci-fi character whose name inspired the design. The usual add-on fittings, such as mirrors, towel bars or soap trays, are built into the frame.

6

7

7 The "Rapsody" washbasin, designed by Berger and Stahl for Rapsel, sets an oval, stainless steel basin in a glass rectangle. This example is finished with a stylish Vola chrome-plated tap – the contemporary architects' favourite choice of fitting for baths and basins.

1 Dornbracht tap fittings line up to show their variety of waterproofed and rust-proofed finishes.

3 The Rubinetterie "Time 95" model is a single-handle mixer tap with a streamlined design.

4 Rubinetterie's "Chantal 27" is a brass and chrome design based on the Edwardian style, with taps and shower nozzle. Taps evolved from this basic cross-bar type to mixers with a central control button to trigger a warm water flow from a central spout.

2 This selection of mixers in chrome is from Vola, a preferred supplier for many architects working worldwide.

5 The award-winning furniture designer Kevin Walz, whose first tap design, "Univers", updates Art Deco, uses chrome and brass trimmings in a hexagonal mixer system.

6 A new design for a Rubinetterie tap, "Ondatris 78" is engineered for function.

9 Børma produces a full range of bathroom accessories to coordinate with their mixer taps, such as this white-lacquered "Lux" tap. This design is also available in both chrome and brass finishes.

7 The Dornbracht mixer tap has an elongated, curved control handle.

8 Gruppo Metals produce "Giro tondo" taps, designed by Davide Mercatali, featuring pop-art imagery in the orbs clustered on the hot and cold water controls set on either side of the spout. Continuing the theme, a single satellite orb is located perched on top of the central mixer spout.

11, 12 & 13 These three taps from the innovative company Gruppo Metals show how to make a basic bathroom fitting more amusing and certainly more colourful. Designers are (left) Edgardo Angelini; (middle) Davide Mercatali; and (right) Roberto Boni.

11

12

13

14

14 An assertive approach in F. A. Porsche's "Eclisse", designed for M. & Z. Rubinetteria.

16

15

15 A very different approach to bathroom fittings is seen here in the spiralling forms of Schmidt-Lackner's design "Roca".

16 "Elemta" from Toni is a simple yet stylish solution to designing single fittings in chrome.

17

10 Art and design combine in this bathroom, designed by architectural company Munkenbeck & Marshall. Artist Danny Lane's custom-built basin shows sculptural form and implicit functionality.

17 Rubinetterie's "Toscane Ponsi" tap is tactile as well as formal. Its form recalls past elegance, while its function is ultra modern.

18 Called "Domani", Italian for tomorrow, this Sieger design regulates the water flow according to the pressure applied to it via a single control.

19

19 Dornbracht reverses the traditional geometry of a tap, making it taller when the thrust of the design is more diagonal in nature.

18

149

1 "Ego", a narcissistic metal-framed dressing table and valet by Renzo de Liberali for StudioLine, features a swivel-drawer storage drum and Carrara marble tabletop.
2 A concrete bathtub, embedded with copper heating coils and functional accessories, preserves the design integrity of an old disused powerhouse converted by architect Gary Cunningham.

6 Carl F. Petersen's smoothly rounded chrome glass holder and soap ring is both unobtrusive and stylish.

1

3 Framed in black and incorporating a scooped bowl light, this Barovier & Toso mirror is a fine example of traditional glass-making techniques working in perfect harmony with modern design.

2

3

4 "Pan", by Turi and Gagliardi for Rapsel, features concentric discs of sanded or painted crystal and a rectangular mirror, supported by a wall-mounted, nickel-plated brass column.
5 Restructured by Andrée Putman, the bathroom at Le Corbusier's Villa Turque incorporates a shaving mirror, with extendable arm and built-in light and magnifying glass, by architect Eileen Gray.

4

5

9

7 Kartell's "Delphi" mirrors, by Mattheo Thun, nonchalantly incline against the wall on rubber grip feet.
8 This chrome-and-plastic soap dish is by Jorge Pensi, from a range of accessories commissioned by Inno to be "rough but in a classical way". Revealing a fine attention to detail, the dish incorporates a channelled and hollowed, clear acrylic insert, which allows water to drain and collect below the soap.
9 This simple circular towel rail is by Agape.

Kitchens

istoric houses open to the public offer the interested observer some glimpses into the life and customs of a by-gone age. As well, they remind us of just how much of that age is now obsolete. The kitchens of these grand, old houses stand as a testimony to changing social custom, the absence of home help, the habit of informal dining, and the development of labour-saving gadgetry that has done so much to fashion our present lifestyles.

Llanhydrock in north Cornwall, England provides a record of the splendour of a late-Victorian kitchen. Barely a century has passed and yet the tools and equipment are now mostly obsolete. Copper jelly moulds hang alongside game hooks; the meat safe stands beside the butler's sink; the marbled dairy room with butter churns offers runnels of icy water in place of refrigeration; the separate laundry, pantry and larder, as well as the dining room beyond the green baize doors, define vividly the way in which today's kitchen space has to take on so

1 A nautical-influenced "porthole" inserted into a kitchen cupboard by Eva Jiricna echoes the viewing window featured on many laundry appliances. **Previous page** Inspired by the patina on steel trucks in Japan, architect John Young specified this unusual finish for stainless steel kitchen units.

2 The matte-black good looks of Roberto Pezzetta's appliances in Zanussi's "Wizard" collection attract deserved attention. The mechanisms are housed in melamine resin, enamelled steel and glass.
3 Architect Johnny Grey specializes in awkward kitchens. "Like a tailor-made suit, the kitchen should fit the house and client," he explains. Craftsmen make everything, even down to cast-iron forged handles.

4 Isolated in the lofty living room in architect Sir Richard Rogers' London home is this free-standing, stainless steel kitchen island. It is a multifunctional installation, and features a double sink unit and a four-plate gas hob. As well, there is a centrally located waste disposal.

6

5

5 Black laminate cabinets by Alno are paired with an update of the traditional butcher's block – a serious cook's tool for chopping and slicing.

6 Strato is a kitchen company dedicated to the research of "the concept of open space". Wood, stone and metal are combined on modular kitchen cabinets. Illuminated by a violet drawer front, this rectangular island has an extension of five metal tubes in the middle of the room, and against the wall a cabinet that houses sinks and appliances.

7 Built in a fairly tight corner, this kitchen by Gwathmey Siegel appears spacious due to clever architectural intervention – reflective tiles bounce back the light from the narrow-panelled, glass-fronted wall that flanks the window with its Venetian blind.

7

1 First appearances deceive with this "Woodline Structure" kitchen from Bulthaup, made entirely from lacquered wood. This complete kitchen features their designed fittings – from the free-standing beech preparation island with drawers to the wire-mesh ceiling fitting.

many different roles as things change. In the 1960s, for example, every kitchen boasted endless casseroles, storage for freeze-dried foodstuffs, and the artificial air of a laboratory inspired by the technology of space exploration.

A change of emphasis in the 1970s produced the idea of the kitchen playing the key role in defining the "quality of life". The kitchen table was central to entertainment, as well as to tasks like homework, and there was a certain homespun air that went with the potted herbs and the use of such "honest" building materials as brick, stone and wood.

Then, in the 1980s, *nouvelle cuisine* launched the cook's kitchen – not only a set of ideas but also a collection of equipment that could shred, extract, pulverize, stir-fry and steam in the most efficient and purposeful of fashions. This gleaming stainless steel room, with its array of architect-designed Alessi

4 This irregularly shaped table, which is curved on one side and has a sharp corner on another, has a tubular-steel support that rests on an aquamarine base. Sensitive spring-touch mechanisms mean that the cabinet doors have no profile in this kitchen of angular contrasts. The good-looking designer stainless steel kitchenware is from Alessi.

2 Unusual finishes on doorfronts with combinations of worktops are a specialty of Miele. Their "Programme 560" has laminated fronts in four pastel shades, shown here in platinum grey, to team with beech worktops, and any one of 130 handles on offer.

3 Woodstock's custom-built "Tracz" kitchen combines maple and coloured sycamore veneered cabinets with a Welsh granite worktop. Spotlights illuminate the essentially duotone coloured room. The octagonal table in the foreground is a space-saving way of accommodating eight diners in a small kitchen area. And beneath the grey floor tiles lies a ducted central heating system.

cookware, made the kitchen the most expensively outfitted space within the contemporary home.

Behind surfaces of steel, enamelled sheet metal and industrial glass teamed with hardwood, cost-effective appliances took the drudgery out of washing, cooking and cooling. The cook's kitchen was one in which every inch of space was taken up by containers, shelves and drawers, with floor and wall cupboards containing all manner of space- and time-saving accessories. Storage carousels, hooks, bins, compartments, wine racks, ice crushers…there was

7 A classic modern design, originally pioneered by Poggenpohl, is this white laminate kitchen by Strato. Stainless steel counters bring this timeless look right up to date. Strato produce modular units that can adapt to different rooms and different needs.

8 Polished metallic lacquer flows over soft curves in this Siematic kitchen, the "SL 808", while segmented marble flooring fans beneath the circular swoop of the worktop.

5 Not just a pretty face – beneath the red lacquer of Miele's "Programme 660" lies a sturdy structure. The high-gloss contemporary finish on a classical frame conceals a stolid particle board carcass.

6 There are 45 door front and handle options, nine front styles, and handles in maple, beech, cherry, chrome and black, within the "Profile 2000" programme from Poggenpohl.

something for every enthusiast. By way of contrast, the busy professional person's kitchen exhibited the new minimalism, with a single, rounded stainless steel bowl, streamlined mixer tap, two-ring gas hob, and a microwave on top of a freezer for convenience food, all set against a background of a slate worktop and anonymous cupboards.

But in today's kitchen this impressive battery of specialized equipment is being refined and relaxed. The current kitchen unbends a little, is less laboratory-like, and is definitely more people-friendly. Dining amid towering banks

155

1 Splitting the functions of cook and bottle-washer and dividing the kitchen territorially is the idea behind Scovolini's briarwood kitchen. The rectangular cabinet, divided by a matte-black extractor hood, houses a built-in oven and hob.

5 Poggenpohl's 2400 "GH" kitchen uses high-gloss laminates to bring the aesthetic quality of their "LH" range to the middle market. Sheer, handle-less fronts feature a polished, horizontal aluminium trim.

3 Effeti's classic "Misura", designed in 1974 by Barsacchi and Vegni, has been brought right up to date with a new proposal from Giancarlo Vegni to utilize all those awkward little corners that are so common in most kitchens.

4 John Young's kitchen gives no signs of cosy domesticity. Stainless steel cabinets with a machined texture and two spring-loaded tables, which can flatten against the wall, allow ample seating for as many as eight people.

2 Even the conventional oven fits gracefully within the curves of this Effeti kitchen, banked in black cabinets that almost appear to float.

of cupboards and aluminium surfaces is not pleasing. Hence the addition of a much-loved piece of old furniture – a kitchen table, perhaps, now scoured to the colour of pale straw, a corner cupboard with carved pediments, or a grandfather clock ticking in a companionable sort of way.

What is more, the reintroduction of these pieces of furniture reflects the new mobility. You can, for example, move them when your circumstances change – a new job, a new apartment, a new relationship. They are not fixed to the wall by installation experts, so you don't have to walk away from all of your kitchen forever.

Every client comes to a kitchen show-room with a basic floor plan. Behind the scenes, however, cooperation between the manufacturers of built-in kitchens and the appliance makers has led to

6 This kitchen has a workbench with a curved end to prevent painful hard knocks. As well, it provides an informal dining bar.

7 Blocks of colour in blues and red stacked in this kitchen, "Logos", from F. lli Ferretti di Ferretto, are grouped under a worktop. The catwalk breakfast bar emphasizes the detailing and the workmanship.

the packaging of kitchens which focus more on designs that will suit the lifestyles and habits of the client.

It is inevitable that in the room where the preparation, cooking and presentation of food is one of the main concerns, together with the washing of plates and the laundering of clothes, appliances are critical to the scheme. The kitchen is by far the most automated room in the home, yet contemporary kitchens tend to confirm that the hearth, or the image of the hearth, is still a cultural icon in today's society. Why else would appliances be disguised behind reassuring wooden fronts that cloak the functional innovations of industrial research?

Technological advances mean that as the energy output of appliances increases, their size reduces. The traditional 23.5-inch (60-cm) square built-in appliance is now available in 18- or 16-inch (45- or 40-cm) sizes without any reduction in workload. In a decade, these appliances have reduced consumption of electricity by 50 percent, of water by 70 percent, and of detergent by 40 percent, and the materials that some are made of make them ecologically disposable. Only the refrigerator continues to grow in size, now acquiring double doors since it is also used as a combination pantry and larder, with a cooled section for wines.

Though not actually coloured green, the thinking behind appliance performance is definitely "green", lurking behind a matte-black mask. "White" goods are undergoing a major technological

8 Kitchens that curve sinuously around corners are a sensible way of providing more storage space without creating the problem of inaccessible far-reaching corners. The new Siematic "9009" kitchen uses polyester in soft curves, aggressively coloured in tomato red or also available in black, ivory or grey.

9 This sharply right-angled kitchen by Sera Noce is in stark contrast with the curved glass-block wall. The kitchen has wooden worktops and splashback with sleek black-lacquered cabinets, and behind the hob a slab of marble provides an effective hard surface.

10 Floor-to-ceiling solid blocks of glossy cabinets are matched by lower, worktop-height cupboards for appliances. The worktop is steel, which, with the glass storage shelves, creates a theatrical space.

11 Blocks of kitchen cabinetry are placed diagonally in this room in an unusual forked-stick design pattern using the new Poggenpohl "Time" range, available in chrome, black, maple, beech or cherrywood.

transformation – instead of hiding behind wooden façades, they are drawing attention to themselves as free-standing objects in their own right.

Ovens, combining steam cooking and special steam pressure cooking with roasting and grilling, are housed in boxes of insulating material that will not adversely affect the furniture on which they sit. So now there is far greater flexibility over where to site them. And the free-standing cooking range, released from the confines of furniture frames, brings the cooker to the focal point of today's kitchen.

The result is the negation of the built-in or fitted kitchen. That line-up of perfectly flush-fitting modular cupboards and units, structurally engineered and then scumbled, rag-rolled and decorated with machine-carved fretwork, is an embarrassing reminder of the new

1 To celebrate the Le Corbusier centenary in 1986, his Villa Turque, built in 1916, was renovated, and interior designer Andrée Putman was commissioned to revive the interiors in the first building ever constructed around a reinforced concrete frame. Putman's company, Ecart, created specific furniture for each space. In the kitchen, one single, free-standing island in stainless steel is covered with three slabs of black maple.
2 A maple top to an island in this chrome-and-laminate Allmilmo "Atlanta" kitchen coordinates well with the wood-block flooring.

3 Proof that high-density particle board is strong enough to support stone is provided in this stacking drawer system from Techline, whose aim, according to Chairman Marshall Erdman, is to "combine quality materials and simple, classic design with the highest technology".

3

7

4

5

4 Corian(R) cleverly combines naturally occurring minerals and acrylic to produce worktop surfaces that can then be edged and shaped to fit seamlessly around sinks. Alno offers Corianware in "Sierra dark" (bottom), "Cameo white" (middle) and "Sierra light" (top).

6 John Pawson's solid slab of grey marble runs the entire length of this kitchen cabinet. In keeping with his minimal interiors, every surface is featureless, without extrusions, curves or fussiness of any sort.

5 Granite is a hard-wearing worktop. Alno, which offers "Sardo rosso" (bottom), "Tiffany black" (middle) and "Nador light" (top) describes the stone as hygroscopic – moisture evaporates without leaving watermarks.

6

7 Marble and stone are popular, if expensive, worktops. Architectural duo Gwathmey Siegel, who use combinations of warm-toned woods in their interiors, replicate that look with a single slab of stone to house the sink.

8 Three solid blocks of marble create a workbench in this kitchen, supported in the middle by a wooden panel. David Chipperfield's architectural pre-occupation with joints is vividly illustrated here in this solid marble worktop, which, despite its obvious weight, gives the impression of somehow floating above what are in themselves substantial side pieces. Delicate grooves, where the worktop meets supporting stones, simply enhance the light and airy effect.

8

opulence and conspicuous consumption. The ideal kitchen these days is fitted out with ecologically conserving appliances, and with them comes a new sense of identity. With everybody in a rush, and with more and more women going to work outside of the home, that traditional picture of the status-symbol kitchen has become something of an anachronism.

There is now more experimentation with styles of eating, too, than was previously the case. People are more adventurous with their cuisine, eating Japanese, Vietnamese, Thai, Malaysian, Californian. And they are also reinterpreting traditional dishes in relation to

1 Salima's "Monoblocci" storage island consists of two base cupboards housed in a laminated wood frame with a worktop for the sink, hob, and plate racks, which can be concealed with a blind when not in use. The kitchen is designed to be compact and self-contained, to suit the smallest apartment.

2 Cooks need to have their utensils easily to hand. Hanging the *batterie de cuisine* on butcher's hooks from a stainless steel rack is Andrée Putman's solution. This stylish interior is a makeover of Le Corbusier's own kitchen in the Villa Turque, which was built in 1916 and refurbished in 1988.

3 The contemporary pantry in Poggenpohl's "Form 2000 CS Vorratsschrank" range has two deep, sliding drawers and a large rotary storage unit that puts provisions within easy reach. Shelf heights are adjustable.

4 Organic waste goes into a green compartment within Alno's plastic triple waste bin, which is fed by a chute from the sink when the cabinet door is closed. Different-coloured bins are used to separate waste products that can be recycled from those that cannot.

5 Open shelving is not always convenient in a kitchen that does double duty as a dining area as well. Poggenpohl's solution is to conceal fixed shelving behind a sliding panel for a quick cover-up.

6 This modern version of a dresser, by architect Michael Carapettan, is designed to house tableware in a small space. It is balanced by recessed worktops with a white-tiled splash-back and granite worktop offering a practical working area.

7 By displaying this handsome collection of cookware on hooks set against black mesh panels, Eva Jiricna has created a contemporary still-life rather than conventional storage.

8 A pair of smoothly contoured columns slide out on runners to reveal food storage in this space-efficient kitchen from Strato, who borrow from grain silo imagery to house provisions.

9 Cooks always accumulate utensils, yet space is finite. This "Esprit" range from Boffi offers a system of horizontal bars to hang shelves at convenient heights for all manner of gadgets.

10 The Museum of Modern Art in New York has exhibited Boffi kitchens, so their design credentials are excellent. But it is for their innovation that they are honoured: the first coloured polyester-finish door, 1954; the first wood and laminate door, 1960; the first door without a handle, 1974; and now with "Dogu", the first kitchen with vertical wooden slats 6 inches (15 cm) wide.

11 Boffi's polyester finish "Xila" range first came into production in 1974, and was the first kitchen with doors that opened with pressure from the top edge of the door, rather than a handle or an indented pull grip.

12 Maple handles with sculpted grips are in fact one of 45 choices available in Poggenpohl's "Form 2000 WP" range.

13 Wasted space is converted into heavy-duty service. All the kitchen base cabinets stand on plinths like skirting boards, and Siematic exploit this space for additional storage that can be opened with a kick.

1 This industrial-style cooking range in white with chrome handles is ranked beside free-standing cabinets and appliances in an imaginative rejection of the fitted kitchen. Sergio Puente unites disparate elements with a soaring, tiled splashback with decorative frieze frame.

2 This handsome Neff "1071 N3" stainless steel oven is pulled forward from the line-up of kitchen cabinets into the room with a work cabinet that sets the hob immediately above the oven.

3 From defrosting to pastry settings – all are easy on this "AKG 334" single oven from Philips Whirlpool.

4 With a stainless steel frame, Ariston's "Gilda" is the first free-standing steam cooker. It has a steam condenser inside, alongside conventional and fan-assisted heat, and a grill.

8 The Siemens dishwasher, positioned beneath a wall-mounted Siemens oven in this Poggenpohl kitchen, can be matched in colour fronts to virtually any kitchen's decorative theme.

modern knowledge concerning nutritional requirements.

With the advent of new functions, the old, claustrophobic kitchen is revealing itself as being too static, too purpose-built. Now it seems that in these more flexible work spaces, which often have to do double duty as dining areas as well, it is no longer a matter of displaying wealth, but rather showing your preference for a quality of life that revolves around shared food, enjoyed in a room where the hand of the architect is not too intrusive.

5 Unlike most advanced ovens, Smeg's "S20XMFR Multi-function" oven has a classic, analogue clock rather than a digital face, understating its high-tech performance.

6 The "Wizard" collection from Zanussi, designed by Roberto Pezzetta, won international acclaim. This oven is styled in matte black and features a horizontal metallic silver handle that blends into the design with six other decorative grey bars, which double as viewports on the black exterior.

7 Offset against a dramatic cobalt blue ground, these white F. lli Ferretti di Ferretto kitchen cabinets house, in a marble worktop, gas burners and a horizontally opening Gaggenau oven.

9 Ariston's "Four Seasons" fridge-freezer is a versatile food-storage system. Its central drawers allow either refrigerator or freezer capacity to be increased. It is also available in white.

10 The kitchen in a converted electricity plant by architect Gary Cunningham is enclosed by a computer-engineered steel-frame structure. Plywood panels were then erected and simply screwed onto cabinets, rather than carefully mitred.

11 Kitchen appliances and fittings are slimmed down in the new Bosch "Concept" series, designed for small-space living. This goes with the growing trend of child-free singles or couples needing less space.

12 John Outram is to British architecture what Steven Spielberg is to the American movie industry – a fantasist who overlays a workable plot with an allegorical and elaborate ornamentation. This kitchen by Outram assembles a battery of appliances – a Miele dishwasher, two Neff ovens plus four gas and four electric rings on the worktop, which is dominated by an extravagantly scaled ventilator hood.

1 Boffi produces stainless steel worktops to support deep sinks and hobs for the professional chef or serious home cook. These steel wells hold Zanussi equipment and fit any Boffi-made kitchen. The aptly named "Gourmet" range is shown here.

2 The "AKG 085" gas hob from Philips Whirlpool has a thin, black skeletal cover and four rings of varying sizes. It can be installed in any type of surface of 1 inch (2.5 cm) depth.

3 In this kitchen by architect David Chipperfield, a square, almost free-standing block for cooking is balanced by a linear one against the wall for dish- and food-washing. The container frames are concrete, the doors walnut, and four powerful rings under an elevated stainless steel rack to cool pans are framed in matte black.

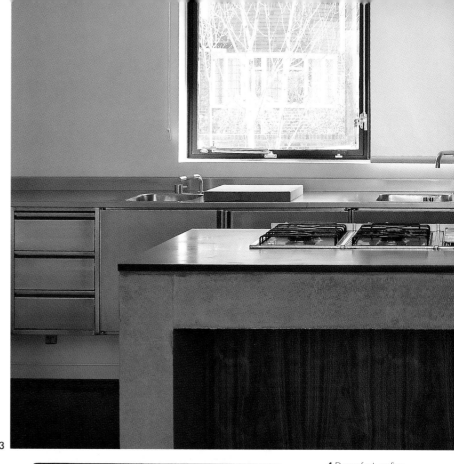

4 Dacor feature five ceramic glass rings, heated by electric elements, star-shaped and in coils, that illuminate the smoky, black-glass, heat-conductive top. The rings are outlined in white, and the controls boldly lit, in this stylish hob unit.

6 This matte-black, four-ring hob from Zanussi's "Wizard" collection, designed by Roberto Pezzetta, features brightly illuminated controls.

7 The Vetroceramic hob from Zanussi uses electric elements and ceramic glass for fast, efficient heat control, with markers from the controls to heat zones.

5 This white Corian worktop features removable stainless steel rods slotted into 3-mm deep grooves. These rods absorb heat and so allow hot pans to be placed on the work surface without any fear of damaging it.

9 Four dual-circuit ceramic heating zones are assembled in an unusual format within the stainless steel hob, model "1094 85NK", by Neff. They co-ordinate with the built-in Circotherm Plus oven with hood in Neff's "Stainless Steel" collection.

10 The imaginative "Piano Ectura Circolare" by Salima features five burners in a semi-circular design, which ensures that pans do not overlap. An added bonus of the design is the free space it creates for either storage or food preparation.

8 In any household the kitchen poses more daily ventilation problems than the bathroom. Bulthaup co-ordinate a stainless steel, four-ringed hob with an overhead stainless steel extractor fan, which can also be used to circulate the air. It features built-in spotlights above the rings, and a hanging bar for utensils.

12 The worktop, like everything else in this kitchen by architect De Maria, is made of granite. Its dramatic circularity of design also makes for easy access.

11 The Italian company Smeg's stainless steel "S93AX" hob is of ample proportions — it is 3 feet (almost 1 metre) long. It is equipped with a fish broiler and ultra-rapid burner to meet the culinary demands of almost any function.

3 This small "Venus" bowl from Avonite can be base-mounted or top recess flush-mounted, making it ideal for custom positioning in any Avonite worktop. Avonite is a man-made, modified polyester sheet material in granite and marble-effect finishes.

4 Villeroy & Boch move away from the traditional ceramic sink to produce a range in a new hard-wearing synthetic material. Although it looks like ceramic, this material has a greater elasticity, which means that there is less chance of breaking pottery and glass. It is also extremely hygienic and easy to clean. This sink with matching draining board is called "Mira", and the colour "Brazil".

2 Low, horizontal planes feature in this spacious kitchen by architects Cecilia and Ottorino Berselli. Custom-cut marble in a long run features a window bay recess and a circular sink, as well as an additional long, shallow, rectangular sink for soaking fish or vegetables.

5 An undermounted bowl in stainless steel from the sink specialists Franke is set into a stylish marble worktop.

1 Ciatti a Tavola's innovative wall-mounted sink makes obsolete the standard base cabinet that supports the conventional sink. Below the shaped marble unit, the plumbing for water and gas and the electrical circuitry is hidden. A tubular-steel rail runs the entire length of the worktop. In this kitchen, storage cabinets and worktops also double up as dining tables.

6 The acrylic material known as Colorcor, shows up different banded colours beneath its durable surface when incised. It has been employed here by architect Eva Jiricna for this grooved drainage board surrounding the deep, rectangular sink set into the worktop.

7

8

7 Made from Siligranit, a composite material composed of granite rock and an acrylic mix, this "Blancostone" sink from Blanco resists scratching, heating, cooling, acids and alkalis. The sink's design offers two bowls, drainage area, china basket, chopping board and waste disposal.

8 Franke's "Compact" sink is designed as a work centre and was developed after research into the demands of the modern cook. A removable chopping board closes off the sink when it is not in use.

9 The Avonite "Athens" sink is a pair of bowls that can be base-mounted or top-recessed flush into any Avonite top, like this one in clean, porcelain white. Avonite can be fused to steel sinks without seams.

9

6

12 An unusually deep bowl, paired like the traditional butler's sinks, is shaped in a contemporary fashion by F. lli Ferretti di Ferretto in white with a grooved draining board.

10

10 & 11 Siematic's sink separates food from cleaning with a shower for washing vegetables in an adjoining bowl. Undersink space is organized with a system of pull-out baskets and bins.

11

12

KITCHENS

1 This versatile "Ladyline" mixer tap from Barking Grohe features many removable, labour-saving attachments, including a pull-out spray, a shower head and a constantly rinsed pan scrubber and bottle brush. An add-on water filter is also available.

2 & 3 Unlike most manufacturers, who make either bowls or taps, Franke combines both functions, thus creating a more integrated product. Two examples are the Franke undermounted bowl (far left and left) for fitting in solid worktops, such as Corian or granite.

4 Pegler's sleek "CD" monoblock mixer is available in chrome, grey, white, beige, mocha red and yellow.

6 Architect Charles Rutherfoord customized this Vola tap, adding industrial on and off knobs. Customizing many types of kitchen accessories is possible, but you will invalidate the manufacturer's guarantee.

7 Blanco's "Borma Lux" chrome mixer tap on a "Blancoprimo" stainless steel sink. Smooth to operate, the tap is also available in white, brass, savanna, beige, platina, brasil and black.

8 This Tantofex "Tantadisc" sink mixer tap with swivel spout is chromium plated, but is also available in gold-plate, white, brown, red, yellow and beige. Hard, ceramic discs provide a permanent, water-tight seal.

5 A bird's-eye view of the "Uranus" sink, made in easy-care, hygienic synthetic material by Villeroy & Boch. The "Europlus" single-lever chrome mixer tap is by Friedrich Grohe.

Directory

Walls & Ceilings

Abet (UK) Ltd
70 Roding Road
London Industrial Park
London E6 4LS
England
Tel: (0171) 473 6910
Fax: (0171) 476 6935
Web Site:
www.abet-laminati.it

Abet Laminati is one of the world's leading manufacturers of high-pressure laminates. With a daily production capacity exceeding 120,000 square metres, its products are distributed worldwide. The company's success is based on technological innovation and collaboration with the design community, and in 1987 Abet was awarded the Compasso d'Oro for Diafos, the world's first translucent laminate. In 1990, Abet Laminati was awarded the European Community Design Prize.

Laminates pp. 22, 23

Blockleys Brick Ltd
Sommerfield Road
Trench Lock
Telford
Shropshire TF1 4RY
England
Tel: (01952) 251 933
Fax: (01952) 641 900
Web Site: www.blockleys.com

Bricks pp. 30, 31

Ceramgres SnC di Fossaluzza C & G
Vic. Spercenigo 21
Mignagola die Carbonera (TV)
Italy
Tel: (0442) 393366
Fax: (0422) 396478

The "Rinascimento" series of tiles is modelled to copy ancient diamond-pointed rustication, with chiaroscuro effects.

Wall and floor tiles

Ceramica Bardelli SpA
Via Pascoli 4/6
20010 Vittuone (MI)
Italy
Tel: (02) 901 11030
Fax: (02) 902 60766
Web Site: www.bardelli.it

Since 1960, Bardelli have manufactured ceramic tiles in Italy. Three fundamental principles characterize their present production line: even colours; the development of sizes; modern graphic design applied to ceramic tiles.

Tiles p. 40

Ceramica Sant'Agostino SpA
Via Statale 247
44047 S. Agostino (FE)
Italy
Tel: (0532) 84 41 11
Fax: (0532) 84 61 13
Web Site: www.netmarket.it/ ceramicasantagostino

Ceramica Sant'Agostino has made floor tiles since 1964 and diversified in the 1970s to make double-fired wall tiles. Their production capacity exceeds 18,000 square metres of tiles a day: 8,000 square metres of enamelled, decorated hardbake and 10,000 square metres of white paste single-fired tiles strengthened with their hard stratos glaze, which is rich in both aluminium and quartz. Continuous research both in classic and contemporary design is making Ceramica Sant'Agostino one of the leading companies in the ceramic tiling field.

Wall and floor tiles

Cotto Veneto Srl
Vic. Tentori 12
31030 Carbonera (TV)
Italy
Tel: (0422) 397791
Fax: (0422) 396537

Cotto Veneto is the trademark of one of the leaders in the manufacture of furnishing ceramics. Glazed tiles, 4 x 4 in (10 x 10 cm) and 2 x 2 in (5 x 5 cm) in size, decorated by hand, include the durable glazed "gres" for floors, kitchens, external coverings and worktops, and glazed strong "Cotto" for kitchen and bathroom floors.

Designers Guild
3 Olaf Street
London W11 4BE
England
Tel: (0171) 243 7320
Fax: (0171) 243 7320
Web Site:
www.designersguild.com

Wallpapers

Dimensione Fuoco Sal
Via V. Veneto 58
30027 S. Dona'di Piave (VE)
Italy
Tel: (0421) 50444
Fax: (0421) 330592

Architects Afra and Tobia Scarpa designed glass screens for Dimensione Fuoco, who revitalized the ancient craft of stained-glass windows, using lead-framed coloured glass with a gilded metal frame.

Windows p.26

Foscarini Murano SpA
Via delle Industrie 92
30020 Marcon (VE)
Italy
Tel: (041) 595 1199
Fax: (041) 595 9232
Web Site: www.foscarini.com

By virtue of its philosophy which sees glass as a means to reach an objective in lighting, Foscarini is far from the Murano tradition which has tended to focus production on aesthetic considerations rather than on functionality. Not a question of renouncing past traditions, Foscarini capitalizes – in a modern key – that inimitable know-how which Murano has bequeathed to the working of glass. So Foscarini's products follow the modernist dictum which advocates the union of function and aesthetics in a single dimension. Widening its original activity in the contract market toward large-scale production for furnishing, Foscarini has transferred into a larger market its experience in pursuing new and original solutions to problems.

Lighting and walls p. 26

Goddard & Gibbs Studios Ltd
41–49 Kingsland Road
London E2 8AD
England
Tel: (0171) 739 6563
Fax: (0171) 739 1979

Domed rooflights and door panels are custom-built in stained glass.

Granitifiandre SpA
Via Radici Nord 112
42014 Castellarano (RE)
Italy
Tel: (0536) 850404
Fax: (0536) 850088
Web Site:
www.granitifiandre.it

As the world's largest producer of porcelain stoneware, Granitifiandre has been used throughout the world on the most prestigious projects. Granitifiandre challenges other ceramic products – marble or natural stone – because its homogeneous, spray-dried mix is composed of the highest quality materials, with exceptional physical properties for durability.

Wall and floor tiles

Hodsoll McKenzie Cloths
52 Pimlico Road
London SW1W 8LP
England
Tel: (0171) 730 2877
Fax: (0171) 254 2033

This firm designs and produces furnishing fabrics and furniture, which are sold at their London showroom.

Kartell SpA
Via delle Industrie 1
20082 Noviglio (MI)
Italy
Tel: (02) 900 121
Fax: (02) 900 91212
Web Site: www.kartell.it

Kartell, founded in the 1950s, is today a leader in the production of plastic furnishings, distinguished from others by collaboration with some of the most famous international designers, including Matteo Thun's mirror collection.

Mirrors p. 150

Klingenberg Dekoramik GmbH
Postfach 1020
8763 Klingenberg/Main
Germany
Tel: (9372) 1310
Fax: (9372) 131220

Founded in 1898, Klingenberg Dekoramik GmbH produce glazed and unglazed, ceramic wall and floor tiles. Today the company is a part of the Division Ceramica Tarkett, with production plants in Italy and Germany. The companies have a good position in export around the world and supply commercial and residential customers.

Langley London Ltd
Harling House
47–51 Great Suffolk Street
London SE1 0SR
England
Tel: (0171) 803 4444
Fax: (0171) 803 4428

Glass blocks

Luxo Italiana SpA
Via delle More
24030 Presezzo (BE)
Italy
Tel: (035) 61 15 62
Fax: (035) 61 01 96
Web Site: www.luxo.com

Interconnected modules like shelves, dado rails or hand rails, even bathroom sets, run along the walls and contain a light source in the "Cornice" series.

"Cornice" light moulding p. 90

A.V. Mazzega Srl
Via Vivarini 3
30141 Murano (VE)
Italy
Tel: (041) 736 677
Fax: (041) 739 939
Web Site: www.avmazzega.com

Glass, produced in the kilns of A.V. Mazzega since 1950, represents the ancient skills of Murano glassblowing giving birth to unique forms, able to catch light and colour in glass blocks and screens for partitions and dividers.

Walls p. 24

Mito Srl
Via Valesana Km 0,560
Zona Industriale
84088 Siano (SA)
Italy
Tel: (081) 518 1085
Fax: (081) 518 1177

Mito Murano Glass tiles, handmade in Venice from a process that is over 1,000 years old, introduced the three-dimensional glass tiles by the artist Lucio Fontana. Molten glass, cast in a mould and hand-shaped, range in tile sizes from 2 x 2 in (5 x 5 cm) to 23 x 23 in (58 x 58 cm) in a variety of shapes. The glass is thick and strong enough for interior and exterior installations as doors, windows or partitions, in private homes or bars, hotels and restaurants. Mito also produces doors and partitions in precious wood for ready installations, as well as exclusive light fittings and mirrors.

Walls pp. 18, 25, 26

Orac Decor
See Muriel Short Designs

Paris Ceramics Ltd
543 Battersea Park Road
London SW11 3BL
England
Tel: (0171) 924 1281
Fax: (0171) 738 0207

Tiles

Perucchetti Associates
RMC House
15 Townmead Road
London SW6 2QL
England
Tel: (0171) 371 5497
Fax: (0171) 371 5842

The ancient art of fresco finishes is revived in contemporary interiors by Mauro Perucchetti Associates, who work closely with designers who commission their special plaster and marble dust walls, with fresco stencilling.

Pilkington Glass Ltd
Prescot Road
St. Helens
Merseyside WA10 3TT
England
Tel: (01744) 692 998
Fax: (01744) 451 326

Pilkington is the name synonymous with glass innovation and panel structural systems in buildings. Their wall "Planar Structural Glazing System" has flexible silicone-sealed joints between panels to provide a complete glass envelope without using frames or mullions so it can be used for vertical, sloping and horizontal applications.

Walls pp. 24, 25, 137

Gruppo Ceramiche Ricchetti Srl
Via Radici in Piano 428
41049 Sassuolo (MO)
Italy
Tel: (0536) 865 111
Tel: (0536) 807 355
Web Site: www.ricchetti.it

Gruppo Ceramiche Ricchetti, together with Klingenberg GmbH in Germany, make up the Ceramic Division of the Swedish Tarkett Group, a worldwide leader in the production of floor and wall covering materials, completing their successful product range of resilient flooring, carpeting and parquet. Ricchetti manufactures ceramic tiles in three production units: Sassuolo (double-fired wall tiles, single-fired white body floor tiles); Fiorano (single-fired frost-proof red body floor tiles); Mordano (single and double-fired wall tiles).

Tiles

Rye Tiles/Rye Pottery
Rye
East Sussex TN31 7DH
England
Tel: (01797) 223 038
Fax: (01797) 224 834
and
12 Connaught Street
London W2 2AF
England
Tel: (0171) 723 7278

Wall and floor tiles

Sadi SpA
Via Olmo, 56
36077 Altavilla Vicenza (VI)
Italy
Tel: (0444) 390 555
Fax: (0444) 390 551

Since 1910, Sadi have produced ceilings in Italy. Now they produce and distribute in the UK, Spain and Japan all kinds of false ceilings, in fibrous plaster, galvanized or stainless steel, aluminium and mineral fibre. They still make interior ornamental plasterwork in accordance with architects' drawings.

Sanderson
100 Acres
Sanderson Road
Uxbridge
Middlesex UB8 1HY
England
Tel: (01895) 238 244
Fax: (01895) 231 450

Wallpaper, fabric and paint

G. Schrattenecker Holzwaren GmbH
Magetsham 19
A-4923 Lohnsburg
Austria
Tel: (7754) 4000
Fax: (7754) 400 140

Tilo, founded in 1952 as a cabinet maker's workshop with only one employee, was by 1991 employing 300, producing mouldings, wooden ceilings, panels and parquets with fine modern technical machines which guarantee top quality.

Panelling p. 28

Muriel Short Designs
Hewitts Estate
Elmbridge Road
Cranleigh
Surrey GU6 8LW
England
Tel: (01483) 271 211
Fax: (01483) 278 317

Mouldings pp. 28, 29

Ingrid Stegmann
Odenwaldstrasse 8
2000 Hamburg
Germany
Tel: (40) 490 4042
Fax: (40) 511 8535

Ingrid Stegmann combines and overlays coloured textures, using up to 15 processes to achieve exclusive paint effects. Her team of artists apply pigment glazes in metallic and pearl finishes, with gold leaf coatings and wax polishes.

Paint design pp. 22, 23

Vortice Ltd
Milley Lane
Hare Hatch
Reading
Berkshire RG10 9TH
England
Tel: (0118) 940 4211
Fax: (0118) 940 3787
Web Site: www.vortice.it

Vortice SpA, established in 1955 in Milan, manufactures domestic and industrial electrical extractor fans, table and ceiling fans and electrical heating appliances. Vortice's products are exhibited in the Museum of Modern Art in New York, La Jolla in Mexico, in Jerusalem, in Munchen, Germany and in the Prato, Florence. They have been awarded design prizes: Compasso d'Oro (Italy), IF-Gute Industrieform (Hannover) and BIO Ljubljana (Slovenia).

Ceiling fans

The York Handmade Brick Co
Forest Lane
Alne
North Yorkshire YO6 2LU
England
Tel: (01347) 838 881
Fax: (01347) 838 885
Web Site:
www.yorkhandmade.co.uk

Bricks

Zanotta SpA
Via V. Veneto 57
20054 Nova Milanese
Italy
Tel: (0362) 368 330
Fax: (0362) 451038
Web Site: www.zanotta.it

Zanotta is one of Italy's respected manufacturers of furniture by the great names in Italian design. Achille Castiglioni is one of the stars in their collection. His movable screens and pivoting stairs give mobile, functional alternatives to more conventional and cumbersome fixtures.

Screens

Floors

P. J. Abrehart
Corner Cottage
Thurvaston
Dalbury Lees
Derby DE6 5BL
England
Tel: (01332) 824 673

American Hardwood Export Council
European Office
10 Throgmorton Avenue
London EC2N 2DL
England
Tel: (0171) 588 8811
Fax: (0171) 588 8855
Web Site: www.ahec.org

Hardwoods from the United States are aggressively marketed throughout the world at this time of ecological consciousness when temperate zone forested timber is preferred to equatorial rainforest hardwoods. Imported into Britain for over a century, the species of hardwood – red oak, white oak, sassafras, cherry, tulipwood, ash, walnut and maple – are also marketed as veneers.

Wood flooring, stairs, window frames

Amtico Company Limited
Kingfield Road
Coventry CV6 5PL
England
Tel: (01203) 861 400
Fax: (01203) 861 552
Web Site: www.amtico.co.uk

Amtico captures the texture of wood, marble, brick and stone in flooring that looks like the real thing, yet is made from durable vinyl sold by the metre. In different colourways, Amtico floor tiles are sold in standard dimensions and thicknesses.

Vinyl, tiles and rolls pp. 35, 37, 45, 138

Artexa SnC di Tosco Ivano & C
Via Roma 116
30030 Pianiga (VE)
Italy
Tel: (041) 519 5201
Fax: (041) 519 5178

A firm started in 1979 for the production of carpets and tapestries, Artexa has gained a stylistic and qualitative reputation in Modern Art carpets in Europe with a vast range of products, made in its own workshops, either by hand or by machine.

Rugs

Azu-Vi SA
Avenida de Italia 58
PO Box 26
12540 Villarreal (Castellon)
Spain
Tel: (964) 509 100
Fax: (964) 509 110

Manufacturer of single-fired glazed tiles decorated with exclusive designs in a wide chromatic range.

Ceramic tiles p. 34

Barbee Ceramics Ltd
Tile Shed
Polhill Garden
London Road
Badgers Mount
Sevenoaks
Kent TN14 7BD
England
Tel and Fax:
(01959) 532 900

Retailers of ceramic tiles from around the world.

Blockleys Brick Ltd
Sommerfield Road
Trench Lock
Telford
Shropshire TF1 4RY
England
Tel: (01952) 251 933
Fax: (01952) 641 900
Web Site: www.blockleys.com

Manufacturers of bricks and decorative paving.

Bosanquet Ives Ltd
3 Court Lodge
48 Sloane Square
London SW1W 8AT
England
Tel: (0171) 730 6241
Fax: (0171) 730 5341

Bosanquet Ives provide a complete carpet service to decorators and specifiers, from design to manufacture and fitting. Specialists in custom-made carpets in

Wilton (velvet pile and Brussels weave) or hand-made as the sole UK agents for Tai Ping, Bosanquet Ives also have many stock ranges of carpets and rugs.

Carpets p. 50

Ceramgres di Fossaluzza C & G SnC
Vic. Spercenigo 21
30130 Mignagola die Carbonera (TV)
Italy
Tel: (0442) 39 33 66
Fax: (0422) 39 64 78

The "Rinascimento" series of tiles is modelled to copy ancient diamond-pointed rustication, with chiaroscuro effects.

Wall and floor tiles

Ceramica Bardelli SpA
Via Pascoli 4/6
20010 Vittuone (MI)
Italy
Tel: (02) 901 11030
Fax: (02) 902 60766
Web Site: www.bardelli.it

Since 1960, Bardelli have manufactured ceramic tiles in Italy. Three fundamental principles characterize their present production line: even colours; the development of sizes; modern graphic design applied to ceramic tiles.

Tiles p. 40

Climpson & Co
Unit 4
Olympia Industrial Estate
Coburg Road
London N22 6TZ
England
Tel: (0181) 881 2211
Fax: (0181) 881 2210

Carpets

Corres Mexican Tiles
1A Station Road
Hampton Wick
Kingston upon Thames
Surrey KT1 4HG
England
Tel: (0181) 943 4142
Fax: (0181) 943 4649

Established in 1951, Corres are the largest company to manufacture hand-made tiles in Mexico. They control, with

a skilled workforce using traditional methods, the entire production and distribution, from quarrying the finest "Barro" (clay) to delivery of the finished product.

Tiles p. 41

Cotto Veneto Srl
Vic. Tentori 12
31030 Carbonera (TV)
Italy
Tel: (0422) 397791
Fax: (0422) 396537

Cotto Veneto is the trademark of one of the leaders in the manufacture of furnishing ceramics. Glazed tiles, 4 x 4 in (10 x 10 cm) and 2 x 2 in (5 x 5 cm) in size, decorated by hand, include the durable glazed "gres" for floors, kitchens, external coverings and worktops, and glazed strong "Cotto" for kitchen and bathroom floors.

Crucial Trading Limited
P.O. Box 11
Duke Place
Kidderminster
Worcestershire DY10 2JR
England
Tel: (01562) 825 200
Fax (01562) 825 177
Web Site:
dspace.dial.pipex.com/crucial

Crucial Trading offer an ever growing collection of natural floor coverings in numerous weaves and colours. Hard-wearing, anti-static and easy to maintain, sisal, coir and seagrass are produced in 4-m latex-backed widths.

Sisal and coir p. 50

Domus Tiles Ltd
33 Parkgate Road
London SW11 4NP
England
Tel: (0171) 223 5555
Fax: (0171) 924 2556
Web Site:
www.domus.tiles.co.uk

Eden Anglo French Ltd
35 Leyton Industrial Village
Argall Avenue
London E10 7QP
England
Tel: (0181) 558 6016
Fax: (0181) 558 9441

Wood and veneer flooring

Egetaepper (UK) Ltd
Ege House
Drumhead Road
Chorley North Business Park
Chorley
Lancashire
England
Tel: (01257) 239 000
Fax: (01257) 239 001

Ege Art-Line carpets, made in Denmark, replicate through the traditional Axminster broadloom weaving process works of art from contemporary artists like Josef Albers and Asger Horn to famous paintings by 20th century artists Paul Klee, René Magritte, Salvador Dalí, and Wassily Kandinsky.

Rugs p. 46

Fired Earth Tile plc
Twyford Mill
Oxford Road
Adderbury
Oxon OX17 3HP
England
Tel: (01295) 812 088
Fax: (01295) 812 832
and
117–119 Fulham Road
London SW3 6RL
England
Tel: (0171) 589 0489

Hand-made floor and wall tiles from Fired Earth include hand-glazed and decorated wall tiles from around the world. Classic floor tiles include a selection of terracottas including reclaimed antique tiles rescued from French châteaux which, though centuries old, are popular in modern interiors, encaustic tiles, mosaics, Venetian marble and slates from Africa, India and China.

Forbo Nairn Ltd
Contract Products Division
PO Box 1
Den Road
Kirkcaldy
Fife KY1 2SB
Scotland
(01592) 643 111
(01592) 643 999
Web Site: www.forbo-nairn.com/contract.htm

Linoleum tiles p. 44

Forbo Nairn Ltd
Leet Court
14 King Street
Watford
Hertfordshire WD1 8BZ
England
Tel: (01923) 238 377
Fax: (01923) 240019
Web Site: www.forbo-nairn/domestic.htm

Gerflor Ltd
Rothwell Road
Warwick CV34 5PY
England
Tel: (01926) 401 550
Fax (01926) 401 647
Web Site: www.gerflor.fr

Vinyls pp. 44, 45

Gerland Ltd
See Gerflor

Granitifiandre SpA
Via Radici Nord 112
42014 Castellarano (RE)
Italy
Tel: (0536) 850404
Fax: (0536) 850088
Web Site:
www.granitifiandre.it

As the world's largest producer of porcelain stoneware, Granitifiandre has been used throughout the world on the most prestigious projects. Granitifiandre spray-dried mix is composed of the highest quality materials, and is exceptionally durable.

Wall and floor tiles

David Gunton Hardwood Floors
Grange Lane
Whitegate Nr. Winsford
Cheshire
England
Tel: (01606) 861 442
Web Sire: www.web-marketing.co.uk/gunton

Haddonstone Ltd
The Forge House
East Haddon
Northampton NN6 8DB
England
Tel: (01604) 770711
Fax: (01604) 770027
Web Site:
www.businessconnections.com/haddonstone

Paving

Hodsoll McKenzie Cloths
52 Pimlico Road
London SW1W 8LP
England
Tel: (0171) 730 2877
Fax: (0171) 254 2033

This firm designs and produces furnishing fabrics and furniture, which are sold at their London showroom.

Junckers Ltd
Wheaton Court Commercial Centre
Wheaton Road
Witham
Essex CM8 3UJ
England
Tel: (01376) 517512
Fax: (01376) 514401
Web Site: www.junckers.com

Junckers, Europe's leading producer of solid hardwood floorings in beech, ash, elm and oak in a wide range of colours, grades and thicknesses, include specialist sports surfaces. Their products include wooden work-tops, chopping boards and a proprietary range of specialist finishing products.

Wood block p. 36

Kievel Stone Ltd
Lower Farm
Ampfield, Nr. Romsey
Hants SO51 9BP
England
Tel: (01794) 368 865
Fax: (01794) 368 914

Natural stone tiles

Kirkstone Quarries Ltd
Skelwith Bridge
Ambleside
Cumbria LA22 9NN
England
Tel: (015394) 33296
Fax: (015394) 34006
Web Sire: www.kirkstone.com

Kirkstone is owned and run by the Fecitt family supported by a skilled workforce of over sixty. Continual investment in updating stone cutting machinery is one of the key factors in Kirkstone's growing success. The capacity for production has steadily increased, and the range of work possible is constantly expanding. Kirkstone Westmorland green slate

has emerged as a designer material, specified by architects and interior designers worldwide.

Slate tiles p. 39

Klingenberg Dekoramik
Postfach 1020
8763 Klingenberg/Main
Germany
Tel: (9372) 131-0
Fax: (9372) 131220

Founded in 1898, Klingenberg Dekoramik GmbH produce glazed and unglazed ceramic wall and floor tiles. Today the company is a part of the Division Ceramica Tarkett, with production plants in Italy and Germany. The companies have a good position in export around the world and supply commercial and residential customers.

Legno Ltd
See Eden Anglo French Ltd

Neotu
25 Rue du Renard
75004 Paris
France
Tel: (1) 42 78 96 97
Fax: (1) 42 78 26 27

Neotu, founded in France in 1985 by Gerard Delmon and Pierre Staudenmeyer, commissions, manufactures and distributes contemporary furniture and soft furnishing like rugs, in limited editions. Designers are chosen for an approach that nourishes references from the past as well as lessons from contemporary art to produce an evolution for the future.

Rugs p. 46

Paris Ceramics Ltd
543 Battersea Park Road
London SW11 3BL
England
Tel: (0171) 924 1281
Fax: (0171) 738 0207

Tiles

Realstone Ltd
Wingerworth
Chesterfield
Derbyshire S42 6RG
England
Tel: (01246) 270 244
Fax: (01246) 220 095
Web Site: www.realstone.co.uk

Natural stone tiles

Reed Harris Ltd
Riverside House
Carnwath Road
London SW6 3HS
England
Tel (0171) 736 7511
Fax: (0171) 736 2988

Marble and granite tiles p. 38

Rowi Parket International BV
PO Box 1033
3430 BA Nieuwegein
The Netherlands
Tel: 3402-60206
Fax: 3402-64174
Web Site: www.rowi.nl

In Holland, Rowi Parket has sold unique hardwood parquet since 1950, exported throughout Europe and to the United States since 1985. Their parquet has a patented installation device to anchor on an underlay varnished, pre-glued, 7-mm thick flooring strips without nails. Newest product launch is the laminate floor replicating pastel-wood and several marble designs.

Wood and laminates pp. 35, 37

Ruckstuhl AG
St. Urbanstrasse 21–31
Postfach 337
CH-4901 Langenthal
Switzerland
Tel: (62) 919 8600
Fax: (63) 919 8690

The Ruckstuhl carpet company in Switzerland, founded in 1881, has never embarked on mass production. To meet the needs of designers, architects and interior decorators, the production of coir, sisal and wool carpets continues to be individual and flexible, while keeping up with technological developments. The co-operation over many years with J.L. Larsen of the USA

culminated in the take-over of the Larsen Carpet Co. which led to the presence of artist Jack Lenor Larsen's carpets in Europe.

Floorcovering p.50

Rye Tiles/Rye Pottery
Rye
East Sussex TN31 7DH
England
Tel: (01797) 223 038
Fax: (01797) 224 834
and
12 Connaught Street
London W2 2AF
England
Tel: (0171) 723 7278

Wall and floor tiles

Saraband Designs
Bath Road
Stroud
Gloucestershire GL5 5ND
England
Tel: (01453) 872 579
Fax: (01453) 872 420

Sisal flooring p. 50

SICIS International
Via Manlio Monti 9–11
48100 Ravenna
Italy
Tel: (0544) 45 13 40
Fax: (0544) 45 14 64

Marbled mosaics produced by modern factory methods is the unique skill of SICIS International, who have patented their method. Specially devised to speed up the ancient craft of hand-laid mosaic floors, the standard pre-assembled, 1-cm thick modules are easily installed.

Mosaic p. 40

Tarkett AB
Box 3004
37203 Ronneby
Sweden
Tel: (457) 71000
Fax: (457) 70528

Vinyl and wood flooring pp. 36, 44, 45

UK outlet:
Tarkett Ltd
PO box 173
Foyle House
Blackthorne Road
Colnbrook
Slough SL3 0AZ
England
Tel: (01753) 765 400
Fax: (01753) 765 448

Toulemonde Bochart SA
ZI de Villemilan
7 Impasse Branly
91320 Wissous
France
Tel: (1) 69 20 40 30
Fax: (1) 69 81 73 12

Founded in the 1940s, Toulemonde Bochart has two important activities: contemporary rugs in wool or synthetic fibres, mechanical or hand-made, and created by famous designers such as Andrée Putman, Jean Michel Wilmotte, Christian Duc, Pascal Mourgue, Emilio Robba and Hilton McConnico, in more than 150 different designs/colours; and the leader in France of wall-to-wall natural fibre coverings like Sisalene, created by Jean Michel Wilmotte.

Rugs p. 47

Vorwerk & Co Teppichwerke KG
Kuhlmannstrasse 11
Export Department
3250 Hamlin
Germany
Tel: (5151) 103-0
Fax: (5151) 103377

While normal, solid-coloured carpet is mostly sold by price and quality, Vorwerk's collections "Dialogues 1 and 2" promote styling. Their star-studded list of artists like David Hockney and Roy Lichtenstein join forces with architects – Sir Norman Foster, Jean Nouvel, Zaha Hadid – to produce the most imaginative collection of boldly patterned carpets for the domestic and contract trade.

Carpets pp. 34, 35, 48, 49

V'Soske Joyce U.K. Ltd
The Clocktower
Coda Centre
Munster Road
London SW6 6AW
England
Tel: (0171) 386 7200

Since 1960, hand-made carpets, custom-designed and custom-sized for fitting in one piece without joints, have been the core business of this Galway-based company, who supply worldwide. "Visions" is their title for a unique collection of limited-edition contemporary works of art, in the medium of hand-tufted rugs and wall-hangings. The medium of hand-tufting is a relatively new addition to the established genre of rugs, tapestries and wall-hangings as an art form.

Rugs p. 47

Wicanders
Amorium (UK) Ltd
Amorium House
Star Road
Partridge Green
Horsham
West Sussex RH13 8RA
England
Tel: (01403) 710 002
Fax: (01403) 710 856
Web Site: www.wicanders-amorium.co.uk

Wicanders are manufacturers and suppliers of an extensive range of cork and wooden floorings, with a reputation for high quality going back over a century.

Cork and wood

The York Handmade Brick Co
Forest Lane
Alne
North Yorkshire YO6 2LU
England
Tel: (01347) 838 881
Fax: (01347) 838 885
Web Site:
www.yorkhandmade.co.uk

Bricks

Doors

G & S Allgood Ltd
297 Euston Road
London NW1 3AQ
England
Tel: (0171) 387 9951
Fax: (0171) 380 1232

Handles

Bd Ediciones de Diseno SA
291 Mallorca
08037 Barcelona
Spain
Tel: (93) 458 6909
Fax: (93) 207 3697

Bd Ediciones de Diseno SA, began in Barcelona in 1972, created by several architects and other professional designers with the intention of producing furniture, objects and accessories for decoration, completely independently, under the direction of architect Xavier Carulla. They make replicas of historic pieces like the door fittings designed in 1914 by Antoni Gaudí, as well as producing the current designs of international designers and architects. Bd Ediciones collaborates with a variety of supply industries, its technology ranging from purely artisanal processes, like those of the Gaudí series, to highly mechanized shelving processes.

Handles

Becchetti Angelo BAL
Via Montini 34
25067 Lumezzane (BS)
Italy
Tel: (030) 826 131
Fax: (030) 828 029

BAL has produced quality solid brass hardware for doors and windows since 1882. Their production range, which includes handles, knobs, hinges, door pulls and knockers and other accessories for interior decoration such as coat hooks, door stops and switch plates, is exported all over the world.

Handles

Clement Windows Group
Clement House
Weydon Rd
Haslemere
Surrey GU27 1HR
England
Tel: (01428) 647 717

Steel door and window frames

Dierre
Strada Statale per Chieri
65/15
14019 Villanova d'Asti (AT)
Italy
Tel: (0141) 94 94 11
Fax: (0141) 94 62 47
Web Site: www.dierre-spa.it

Dierre specialize in armoured doors, producing 70,000 annually which places it among one of the top 50 fast-growing companies in Italy. In this security-conscious age, the group has developed – and produced – locks, armoured fire-proof doors, steel shutters and safes.

D-Line Intl
Carl Jacobsens Vej
1790 Copenhagen V
Denmark
Tel: (36) 180 400
Fax: (36) 180 401
Web Site: www.dline.com

D-Line, manufactured by Carl F. Petersen in Denmark, is a range of high-quality stainless steel or polished brass fittings which meets practically every requirement within a building – not only for doors, windows and bathrooms but interiors in general.

Handles p.64
see also Bathrooms, p. 150

Eurobrass SrL
Via Brescia 104
25076 Odolo (BS)
Italy
Tel: (0365) 860761
Fax: (0365) 860887

Eurobrass, established in 1985 to produce solid brass products, has made its presence felt across Europe and America, with door handles designed by architect Giuseppe Raimondi, marketed under the "Designer Collection" label.

Handles

FSB
See Franz Schneider Brakel

Handles and Fittings Ltd
HAF House
Mead Lane
Hertford
Hertfordshire SG13 7AP
England
Tel: (01992) 505 655
Fax: (01992) 505 705
Web Site:
www.giant.co.uk/hfl.html

Specialists in architectural ironmongery, Handles and Fittings Ltd introduced three ranges of contemporary door furniture which was extended to encompass bathroom accessories, electrical fittings, door closers and locks, all made exclusively for them in England.

Handles

Lualdi Porte SpA
Via Brigate di Dio
20010 Mesero (MI)
Italy
Tel: (02) 9789 248
Fax: (02) 9728 9463

Lualdi Porte began door manufacturing in 1960, the first firm to introduce designers and the first to produce polyester lacquered doors. Their doors are distributed worldwide.

Mandelli & C SpA
Via Rivabella 90
20045 Besana Brianza (MI)
Italy
Tel: (0362) 949755
Fax: (0362) 949759
Web Site: www.mandelli.it

Italian Mandelli & C manufacture door handles. Fashion plays an important role in its line of brass door fittings, and some classic ranges are still made as a consequence of contemporary tastes. An assortment of handles and door accessories is available in brass, bronze, copper, gold-black and 24-carat gold plate, all with the exclusive "Fluxcoating" system to assure longer wear. Mandelli hardware is now available in more than 34 countries.

Handles

Carl F. Petersen
See D-Line Intl

Franz Schneider Brakel GmbH & Co
PO Box 1440
33029 Brakel
Germany
Tel: (5272) 6080
Fax: (5272) 608302

The architectural hardware of FSB reflects the "Zeitgeist" of more than 100 years since the FSB company was formed in 1881 by Franz Schneider in a small town in an areas called the "Weserbergland" in Germany. FSB produces architectural hardware made of aluminium, stainless steel, brass and bronze for doors, windows and furniture. To bring new ideas to the market, FSB invited important architects and designers around the world to present their ideas for a new design for the 1990s. Many participated, among them Arata Isozaki, Dieter Rams, Peter Eiseman, Mario Botta, Alessandro Mendini and Jasper Morrison.

Handles

Sellex S.A.
Donosti Ibildea 84
Poligono 26
20115 Astigarra-Ergobia (GU)
Spain
Tel: (943) 557 011
Fax: (943) 557 040
Web Site: www.sidi.es/sellex

Sellex was established in 1977 and produces and markets modern design furniture and accessories in collaboration with most famous Spanish designers. Sellex has been a member of SIDI Group since it was created in 1984 and in 1987 was the first company in Spain to organize a National Design Competition.

Handles

Tecnolumen Walter Schnepel GmbH
Loetzener Str. 2–4
2800 Bremem
Germany
Tel: (421) 444 016
Fax: (421) 498 6685

Tecnolumen is the producer of hardware accessories, designed in the 1920s and 1930s by famous designers including members of the Bauhaus School. Tecnolumen is the sole licensee of the respective designs and also the producer of contemporary designs by architects.

Handles

Tre-Piu SpA
Via V. Veneto 14/16
20060 Cabiate (CO)
Italy
Tel: (031) 76 60 00
Fax: (031) 76 83 83

The Tre-Piu door company was founded in 1982 arising from a merger between a large door-manufacturing company "Tre-P SpA" of Birone di Guissano, and a furniture manufacturer who had been present on the furnishing market for three generations, Santambrogio of Cabiate. The Tre-Piu company ("piu" i.e. "more") means in this case three more, producing door designs commissioned by designers and architects. Hinged doors, sliding and folding doors, even security doors are produced with attention to detail, and a final application of the glossy polyester varnish.

Valli & Colombo
See Valli & Valli

Valli & Valli
Via Concordia 16
20055 Renate (MI)
Italy
Tel: (0362) 982 260
Fax: (0362) 924 455

Since 1934, Valli & Valli has been a leading company at international level in the production of handles and decorative fittings in high quality brass. Their wide range includes different models divided into three collections: "Classic", "Design" and "Casual".

Handles

Yannedis Ltd
Riverside House
Southend Road
Woodford Green
Essex IG8 8HQ
England
Tel: (0181) 550 8833
Fax: (0181) 551 0026

Yannedis and Company Ltd, the British architectural hardware firm, was established in 1911 and has six branches in England and three subsidiary companies. They specialize in modern door furniture from Italy and Germany and in handrails, balustrading, electrical accessories and grilles.

Handles

Windows

American Hardwood Export Council
European Office
10 Throgmorton Avenue
London EC2N 2DL
England
Tel: (0171) 588 8811
Fax: (0171) 588 8855
Web Site: www.ahec.org

Hardwoods from the United States are aggressively marketed throughout the world at this time of ecological consciousness when temperate zone forested timber is preferred to equatorial rainforest hardwoods. Imported into Britain for over a century, the species of hardwood – red oak, white oak, sassafras, cherry, tulipwood, ash, walnut and maple – are also marketed as veneers.

Wood flooring, stairs, window frames

Celia Birtwell
71 Westbourne Park Road
London W2 5QH
England
Tel: (0171) 221 0877
Fax: (0171) 229 7673

Fabric sheers

Clement Windows Group
Clement House
Weydon Rd
Haslemere
Surrey GU27 1HR
England
Tel: (01428) 647 717

Steel window frames

Dimensione Fuoco Sal
Via V. Veneto 58
30027 S. Dona'di Piave (VE)
Italy
Tel: (0421) 50444
Fax: (0421) 330592

Architects Afra and Tobia Scarpa designed glass screens for Dimensione Fuoco, who revitalized the ancient craft of stained-glass windows, using lead-framed coloured glass.

Windows p.26

Dimes SpA
Via Provinciale per Modena 49
41016 Novi di Modena (MO)
Italy
Tel: (059) 670155
Fax: (059) 676341
Web Site:
www.dimes-scale.com

Dimes in Italy, producers of staircases and attic windows for more than 25 years in quality materials, manufactures folding, open spiral and modular staircases.

Staircases

Foscarini Murano SpA
Via delle Industrie 92
30020 Marcon (VE)
Italy
Tel: (041) 595 1199
Fax: (041) 595 9232
Web Site: www.foscarini.com

By virtue of its philosophy which sees glass as a means to reach an objective in lighting, Foscarini is far from the Murano tradition which has tended to focus production on aesthetic considerations rather than on functionality. Not a question of renouncing past traditions, Foscarini capitalizes – in a modern key – on that inimitable know-how which Murano has bequeathed to the working of glass. So Foscarini's products follow the modernist dictum which advocates the union of function and aesthetics in a single dimension. Widening its original activity in the contract market toward large-scale production for furnishing, Foscarini has transferred into a larger market its experience in pursuing new and original solutions to problems.

Lighting and walls p. 26

Harris Fabrics Ltd
Bradbourne Drive
Tilbrook
Milton Keynes MK7 8BE
England
Tel: (01908) 366922
Fax: (01908) 370389

Corduroy

Leoplast SrL
Via Po 1
53036 Poggibonsi (SI)
Italy
Tel: (0577) 936 722
Fax: (0577) 939 988
Web Site: www.leoplast.it

Leoplast has been manufacturing PVC window blinds since 1958. Its range now includes rolling shutters, wall linings, folding doors, sliding panel blinds and lifting blinds.

Blinds

Mary Fox Linton Ltd
Chelsea Harbour Design Centre
London SW10 0XE
England
Tel: (0171) 351 9908

Fabrics

The Louvre Blind Company Ltd
7 Forward Drive
Harrow
Middlesex
HA3 8NT
England
Tel: (0181) 863 9111
Fax: (0181) 863 8760

Windows p.74

Mito Srl
Via Valesana Km 0,560
Zona Industriale
84088 Siano (SA)
Italy
Tel: (081) 518 1085
Fax: (081) 518 1177

Mito Murano Glass tiles, handmade in Venice from a process that is over one thousand years old, introduced the three-dimensional glass tiles by the artist Lucio Fontana. Molten glass, cast in a mould and hand-shaped, range in tile sizes from 2 x 2 in (5 x 5 cm) to 23 x 23 in (58 x 58 cm) in a variety of shapes. The glass is thick and strong enough for interior and exterior installations as doors, windows or partitions, in private homes or bars, hotels and restaurants. Mito also produces doors and partitions in precious wood for ready installations, as well as exclusive light fittings and mirrors.

Walls pp. 18, 25, 26

Monarch Aluminium Ltd
Rutherford Way
Manor Road
Cheltenham
Gloucestershire GL51 9SQ
England
Tel: (01242) 510554
Fax: (01242) 576 258
Web Site: www.granges.co.uk

Monarch, trading under the name of Eden and one of the UK's biggest manufacturers of conservatories and greenhouses, introduce canopies for carports that combine strong yet light-weight aluminium with design, for easy DIY installation without specialized equipment.

Navello SpA
Via G. Cappa 24
12063 Dogliani (CN)
Italy
Tel: (0173) 70 132
Fax: (0173) 70 663
Web Site:
www.areacom.it/biz/navello

Navello produce a variety of wooden window frames using mostly Swedish Douglas Pine, which are marketed together with fitting roller blinds, conventional and sliding shutters and blinds.

Rea Metal Windows Ltd
Knowsley Works
Green Lane
Stanley
Liverpool L13 7ED
England
Tel: (0151) 228 6373
Fax: (0151) 254 1828

Rea have operated at Merseyside UK as specialist manufacturers and installers of windows and doors since 1906, the first company in the UK to be awarded the BSI Kite Mark for steel windows. Since 1974, Rea have also manufactured windows and doors from Swiss cold-formed tubular steel profiles. Products from this range include standard construction insulating and non-insulating fire-rated construction security windows and steel frame curtain walling.

Sahco Hesslein
Chelsea Harbour Design Centre
London SW10 0XE
England
Tel: (0171) 352 6168

Textiles p. 76

Sander-Shade
Unit 8, Treadaway Tech Centre
Loudwater
High Wycombe
Buckinghamshire HP10 9RS
England
Tel: (01628) 529 676
Fax: (01628) 521 684

Blinds

Silent Gliss ltd
Star Lane
Margate
Kent CT9 4EF
England
Tel: (01843) 863 571
Fax: (01843) 864 503
Web Site:
www.silentgliss.com

Tracks

Standard Patent Glazing Co Ltd
Forge Lane
Dewsbury
Yorkshire WF12 9EL
England
Tel: (01924) 461 213

Roof glazing, skylights

Swift Blinds
Aldon Works
177 Lockwood Road
Huddersfield HD1 3TG
England
Tel: (01484) 512741
Fax: (01484) 542954

Blinds

Tidmarsh & Sons
32 Hyde Way
Welwyn Garden City
Al7 3AW
England
Tel: (01707) 886 226
Fax: (01707) 886 227

Blinds

Varia Textile Limited
197 Kings Road
Kingston upon Thames
Surrey KT2 5JH
England
Tel: (0181) 549 8590
Fax: (0181) 549 8290

Varia designer accessories include curtain rods and fittings supplied in a variety of beautiful finishes from traditional brass and wood to Art Deco nickel and black.

Vertika International Ltd
PO Box 66
Macclesfield
Cheshire SK11 7PR
England
Tel: (01625) 611 622
Fax: (01625) 612 616

Blinds

Zimmer & Rohde
Chelsea Harbour Design Centre
London SW10 0XE
England
Tel: (0171) 351 7115

Fabrics p. 76

Stairs

Albini & Fontanot SpA
Via P. Pasolini 6
47040 Cerasolo Ausa (RI)
Italy
Tel: (0541) 75 94 55
Fax: (0541) 75 95 45

Albini & Fontanot climbed to brand leader in stairs many years ago, and use steel, wood and polyurethane for their architecturally planned stairways.

Stairs pp. 81, 83, 84

Boundary Metal
Building 195
New Greenham Park
Newbury
Berkshire RG19 6HL
England
Tel: (01635) 42 255
Fax: (01635) 528 432

Architectural metal work includes mild steel and wrought iron balustrades, fixings and component parts for stairs and fire escapes with detailing in brass or epoxy-coated colour.

Dimes SpA
Via Provinciale per Modena 49
41016 Novi di Modena (MO)
Italy
Tel: (059) 670155
Fax: (059) 676341
Web Site:
www.dimes-scale.com

Dimes in Italy, producers of staircases and attic windows for more than 25 years in quality materials, manufactures folding, open spiral and modular staircases.

Staircases

HEWI (UK) Ltd
Scimitar Close
Gillingham Business Park
Gillingham
Kent ME8 0RN
England
Tel: (01634) 377 688
Fax: (01634) 370 612
Web Site: www.martex.co.uk

Stairs p. 81

Nusteel Structures Ltd
Lympne
Hythe
Kent CT21 4LR
England
Tel: (01303) 268112
Fax: (01303) 266098

Balustrades for John Young's Thamesreach Apartment.

Stairs p. 84

Secco Sistemi SpA
Via Terraglio 195
31022 Preganziol (TV)
Italy
Tel: (0422) 38 13 81
Fax: (0422) 38 26 43

Secco Sistemi SpA is the leading manufacturer of cold-rolled products for windows, doors and curtain walling.

Heating

Alessi F.A.O. SpA
Via Privata Alessi 6
28022 Crusinallo (VB)
Italy
Tel: (0323) 86 86 11
Fax: (0323) 64 16 05
Web Site: www.alessi.it

Alessi, the Italian manufacturers of stainless steel with style, has a high company profile worldwide for its products commissioned from internationally acclaimed architects and designers. No designer kitchen was without an Alessi kettle by Michael Graves or Richard Sapper, and now their heating and fireplace accessories may take over the hearth.

Fireplace accessories p. 100, see also Kitchens, p. 154

Atelier Dominique Imbert Sarl
Le Fort
34380 Viols le Fort
France
Tel: (4) 67 55 01 93
Fax: (4) 67 55 77 77
Web Site:
www.focus-creation.com

"Focus" is the trade-mark of a range of contemporary fireplaces with vents and chimneys, sold throughout Europe, in Japan and Canada, mainly to architects and interior designers.

Fireplaces pp. 98, 100

Avant Scene
4 Place de l'Odéon
75006 Paris
France
Tel: (1) 46 33 12 40
Fax: (1) 46 33 92 78

Avant Scene was founded in 1986 in the spirit of a new approach to interiors to present the furniture and objects designed by young sculptors and artists, mostly French, who participated in the "Renaissance" of an appreciation of modernity.

Fireplace accessories p. 102

Benn-Gurleyik Design Studio
Markgroeninger Strasse 61
Stuttgart
Germany
Tel: (711) 870 2105
Fax: (711) 870 2106

This dynamic young design studio in Germany comprises a multi-lingual staff catering for international clients in industry, production, lighting, furniture and packaging, and facilities which develop 3-D models from an early stage through to finished prototypes.

Bisque Ltd
244 Belsize Road
London NW6 4BT
England
Tel: (0171) 328 2225
Tel: (0171) 328 9845

Bisque invented the concept of the "Designer Radiator", selling heating which marries form and function. A great diversity of shapes and sizes are available in hundreds of colours, some also in metallic finishes.

Radiators pp. 93, 96

Calor Gas Ltd
Appleton Park
Riding Court Road
Datchet, Slough
Berkshire SL3 9JG
England
Tel: (01753) 40000
Fax: (01753) 586037
Web Site: www.calor.com

Nationwide gas information service and product listing in Britain.

Caradon Heating Ltd
PO Box 103
National Avenue
Hull HU5 4JN
England
Tel: (01482) 492251
Fax: (01482) 448858
Web Site: www.caradon.com

Stelrad Ideal are heating products by Caradon.

Cosybug Ltd
See Harton Heating Appliances Ltd

Dimplex Heating
Manor House Avenue
Millbrook
Southampton SO9 2DP
England
Tel (01704) 777 117
Fax: (01704) 704 096

In Britain since 1955, Dimplex has lined up new designs in coloured electrical heating with "real flame" effect fires, powerful fan storage heaters and oil-filled radiators, and mobile air conditioning units.

Heating p. 102

Electricity Association
30 Millbank
London SW1P 4RD
England
Tel: (0171) 963 5700
Fax: (0171) 963 5959
Web Site:
www.electricity.org.uk

Promotions board for electricity offering consumer consumption advice.

Elgin & Hall Ltd
Adelphi House
Hunton
Bedale
North Yorkshire DL8 1LY
England
Tel: (01677) 50712
Fax: (01677) 50713

Elgin & Hall began reproducing famous period mouldings and fireplaces with specialist finishes to suit contemporary living. Their elegant fireplace surrounds that look to Louis XVI, but in 1990s matte-black, are produced in limited editions for contemporary interiors.

Fireplaces p. 100

Flamewave Fires
Branbridges Road
East Peckham
Kent TN12 5HH
England
Tel: (01622) 872579
Fax: (01622) 872721
Web Site:
www.flamewavefires.co.uk

Fireplaces

Harton Heating Appliances Ltd
(Incorporating Cosybug Ltd)
Unit 6
Thistlebrook Industrial Estate
Eynsham Drive
Abbey Wood
London SE2 9RB
England
Tel: (0181) 310 0421

Specialists in metal heating
units and boilers for
architectural projects.

Philip Hearsey FCSD
Monkhall Court
Callow
Hereford HR2 8DA
England
Tel: (01432) 351170
Fax: (01432) 354162

Philip Hearsey's hand-forged
design work, predominantly
concerned with architectural
and interior projects for both
corporate and private clients,
includes firebacks, hoods
and baskets.

Fireplace accessories

Magnificent Marble
High Street
Sutton
Surrey
England
Tel: (0181) 643 1723

Magnificent Marble
manufactures fireplaces and
hearths, kitchen worktops,
and bathroom vanity tops and
both bath and wall panels in
marble and granite at their
workshop and showroom in
Surrey. The company, which
began in 1989, offers a
design, manufacturing and
fitting stonemasonry service
to interior designers.

Fireplaces

Marble Hill Fireplace
70/72 Richmond Road
Twickenham
Middlesex TW1 3BE
England
Tel: (0181) 892 1488
Fax: (0181) 891 6591

Fireplaces, radiator covers

Rega Metal Products
Station Road
Sandy
Bedfordshire SG19 1BH
England
Tel: (01767) 691 291
Fax: (01767) 692 451

*Heating and ventilation
products*

Runtal Italia SrL
Via del Lavoro 14
20069 Pozzo d'Adda (MI)
Italy
Tel: (2) 9096 8440
Fax: (2) 9096 8402

Runtal Italia, licensee of the
Swiss company, offers 18,000
radiator models which vary in
length, depth and breadth in
160 colours.

Heating p. 94, 95, 96

Stelrad
PO Box 103
National Avenue
Hull
North Humberside
England
Tel: (01482) 492251
Web Site: www.caradon.com

Fireplaces pp. 94, 95

Thermocet UK
Bower and Childs
91 Wakefield Road
Huddersfield HD5 9AB
England
Tel: (01484) 425 416

Heating p. 99

Trox Brothers Ltd
Hewitt Road
Gapton Hall Industrial Estate
Great Yarmouth
Norfolk NR31 0NL
England
Tel: (01493) 652 947
Fax: (01943) 441 164

Trox Brothers, manufacturers
in the UK of ventilation
systems, use steel and plastic
construction for grille facings.

Ventilation

Wirsbo (UK) Ltd
Space House
Satellite Business Village
Crawley
West Sussex RH10 2NE
England
Tel: (01293) 548 512
Fax: (01293) 548 522

Heating, radiators

Zehnder-Beutler GmbH
Almweg 34
77933 Lahr
Germany
Tel: (7821) 586 0
Fax: (7821) 52553

Zehnder's Arcus, the
contemporary design by Prof.
Bitsch and Partners of a
combined radiator and towel
heater, comes in a great
variety of colours and colour
combinations, widths and
heights. Arcus can be used
with an existing central
heating system or electricity.
The metal bars are arranged
horizontally resembling
ladders rather than radiators.

Heating pp. 94, 95, 97

UK outlet:
Zehnder (UK) Ltd
Invincible Road
Farnborough
Hants GU14 7QU
England
Tel: (01252) 515 151
Fax: (01252) 522 528

Lighting

Arteluce
McInnes Cook
31 Lisson Grove
London NW1 6UV
England
Tel: (0171) 258 0600
Fax: (0171) 523 7005

Arteluce began producing
lamps and testing technology
and new materials in the
1930s. Then, the business
was aimed at contracts for
hotels, schools and offices.
In 1974, Arteluce was taken
over by Flos, who updated
production with lighting
fixtures and systems suitable
for both residences and the
contract market. Now
Arteluce anticipates new
trends and creates
sophisticated environments.

Lighting p. 109

Artemide GB Ltd
106 Great Russell Street
London WC1B 3DG
England
Tel: (0171) 631 5200
Fax: (0171) 631 5222
Web Site:
www.artemide.co.uk

Lighting p. 109

Belux AG
Bremgarterstrasse 109
CH 5610 Wohlen
Switzerland
Tel: (56) 618 7373
Fax: (56) 618 7327
Web Site: www.belux.ch

Belux began developing and
producing lights for offices
and workshops in the 1970s.
Quality and durability were
always the requirements, and
today's lights integrate the
latest technologies in industrial
manufacture. In 1982 Belux
invented the suspended light
system, "Metro", and in 1989
the new plug-in light system,
"Contacto", followed. In 1984
Belux launched a design
competition, with a jury
including Achille Castiglioni,
Robert and Trix Haussmann,
and Margot Weinberg-Staber.
For this competition Benjamin
Thut designed the successful
pivoting light "Lifto" which
received several awards.

Lighting p. 111

UK outlet:
Lumino Limited
Lovet Road
Harlow
Essex CM19 5TB
England
Tel: (01279) 635 411
Fax: (01279) 626 101
Web site: www.lumino.co.uk

Blauet S.A. (Grupo Sidi)
Aragón 333
08009 Barcelona
Spain
Tel: (93) 207 53 11
Fax: (93) 207 33 98
Web Site: www.blauet.com

Founded in Barcelona in
1983 to produce and
distribute lighting designs,
Blauet have rapidly gained
a distinctive profile and
awards for their pendant
standard and table lights.

B.LUX S.A.
Polig.Eitua, S/N
48240 Berriz (Vizcaya)
Spain
Tel: (94) 682 72 72
Fax: (94) 682 49 02

Fifteen years experience in the
making and sales of modern
lights, with an international
team of designers, makes
Spanish B.LUX an
international award winner,
with outlets in Germany, USA,
Benelux, France, Italy, Japan,
as well as Scandinavia. Their
UK outlets include Candell
Lighting in Muswell Hill,
London.

Anglepoise Ltd
Enfield Industrial Area
Redditch B97 6DR
England
Tel: 01527 63771
Fax: 01527 61232

Manufacturers of Anglepoise
lamps.

Busch-Jaeger Elektro GmbH
Postfach 1280
58505 Lüddenscheid
Germany
Tel: (2351) 9 560
Fax: (2351) 9 56694
Web Site:
www.busch-jaeger.de

Busch-Jaeger is a manufacturer of electrical installation material. The company group consists of three plants located in Germany – Luedenscheid (the principal place of business), Aue and Hamm – and in addition holding companies in Spain and Finland as well as a production site in Singapore. The company manufactures more than 6000 classic, as well as technologically innovative, electrical products.

Candela Ltd
Unit 51
Abbey Business Centre
Ingate Place
London SW8 3NS
England
Tel: (0171) 720 4480
Fax (0171) 498 0026

Established in 1982, the English company Candela Ltd designs, manufactures and markets the new generation of lights – low voltage, tungsten halogen, reflector lamps – for architectural and display lighting.

Lighting p. 110

Candell Lighting Ltd
20/22 Avenue Mews
Muswell Hill
London N10 3NP
England
Tel: (0181) 444 9004
Fax: (0181) 444 5232

UK outlet for B.LUX S.A.

Catalytico UK
25 Montpelier Street
London SW7 1HF
England
Tel: (0171) 225 1720
Fax: (0171) 225 3740

UK stockists for Ingo Maurer, LucePlan and Foscarini Murano.

Clipsal (UK) Ltd
The Merlin Centre
Cressex Business Park
Lancashire Road
High Wycombe
Buckinghamshire HP12 3QL
Middlesex HA7 1DA
England
Tel: (01494) 523 333

Clipsal, market leader in electrical accessories throughout Australasia and Asia, have manufactured electrical accessories in Australia since 1920, and in Britain, markets and comprehensive range of stylishly coloured switches and sockets.

Light switches

Concord Lighting Ltd
174 High Holborn
London WC1V 7AA
England
Tel: (0171) 497 1400
Fax: (0171) 497 1404

Concord Lighting is Britain's leading manufacturer of architectural display lighting, selling in 65 countries, with lighting ranges including low-energy downlighters and a range of high-performance downlighters.

Lighting pp. 107, 108, 109

Davey Lighting
1 Chelmsford Road Industrial Estate
Great Dunmow
Essex CM6 1HD
England
Tel: (01371) 873 174

Suppliers of marine, industrial and transport lighting.

ERCO Lighting Ltd
38 Dover Street
London W1X 3RB
England
Tel: (0171) 408 0320
Fax: (0171) 409 1530
Web Site: www.erco.com

ERCO's objective of selling light, not lights, has been realized both in terms of know-how and of actual products. Working on the perception that light is the fourth dimension of architecture, a range of products has been developed that can be utilized in areas of architecture and illumination. An important element in this process is the need to integrate light, and thus light fittings, into the architecture.

Lighting p. 108

Estiluz SA
Ctra Ogassa s/n
17860 Sant Joan de les Abadesses (Gerona)
Spain
Tel: (97) 2720125
Fax: (97) 2720796
Web Site:
www.arrakis.es/~estiluz

Estiluz, a Spanish company designing and manufacturing halogen light fittings from 1969 in its own production plant in collaboration with external experts, has penetrated European, US and Canadian markets.

Fabbian SpA
Via S. Brigida 50
31020 Castelminio Di Resana (TV)
Italy
Tel: (0423) 784535/6/7
Fax: (0423) 484395
Web Site: www.fabbian.it

Fabbian Lighting is represented at major markets, and company expansion occurs alongside precise commercial development. Strong technological knowledge of metal and glass processing, detailed design, and safety testing of electrical fixtures and fittings for each country's requirements take Fabbian products worldwide.

Flos Lighting Fixtures
McInnes Cook
31 Lisson Grove
London NW1 6UV
England
Tel: (0171) 258 0600
Fax: (01977) 723 7005

In the 1960s, Flos began manufacturing their lighting fixtures to a very high design standard. The company aims not only at the innovative aspects of design, but also to produce models that will stand the test of time: a great number of the first thirty models produced are still in the catalogue today, proving that the techniques and forms chosen in the past are still up-to-date and functional. They use materials as different as marble, glass, metals and plastics to meet the latest advances in technology and the safety standards imposed by the national and international markets.

Forma Lighting Ltd
Unit 3
Mitcham Industrial Estate
85 Streatham Road
Mitcham
Surrey CR4 2AP
England
Tel: (0181) 640 6811
Fax: (0181) 640 6910

UK distributors of Italian decorative lighting, specializing in Murano glass.

Foscarini Murano SpA
Via delle Industrie 92
30020 Marcon (VE)
Italy
Tel: (041) 595 11 99
Fax: (41) 595 92 32
Web Site: www.foscarini.com

By virtue of its philosophy which sees glass as a means to reach an objective in lighting, Foscarini is far from the Murano tradition, which has tended to focus production on aesthetic considerations rather than on functionality. Not a question of renouncing past traditions, Foscarini capitalizes – in a modern key – on that inimitable know-how which Murano has bequeathed to the working of glass. So Foscarini's products follow the modernist dictum which advocates the union of

function and aesthetics in a single dimension. Widening its original activity in the contract market toward large-scale production for furnishing, Foscarini has transferred into a larger market its experience in pursuing new and original solutions to problems.

Lighting and walls p. 26

Rod Hamilton & Co Ltd
Quarry Industrial Estate
Mere Warminster
Wiltshire BA12 6LA
England
Tel: (01747) 860 088
Fax: (01747) 861 032
Web Site:
www.rhamilton.co.uk

Lighting accessories and control systems

Handles and Fittings Ltd
HAF House
Mead Lane
Hertford
Hertfordshire SG13 7AP
England
Tel: (01992) 505 655
Fax: (01992) 505 705
Web Site:
www.giant.co.uk/hfl.html

Specialists in architectural ironmongery, Handles and Fittings Ltd introduced three ranges of contemporary door furniture which was extended to encompass bathroom accessories, electrical fittings, door closers and locks, all made exclusively for them in England.

Handles

IGuzzini Illuminazione UK Ltd
Unit 3
Mitcham Industrial Estates
85 Streatham Road
Mitcham
Surrey CR4 2AP
England
Tel: (0181) 646 4141
Fax: (0171) 640 6910

UK distributors of Italian lighting.

Ingo Maurer GmbH
47 Kaiserstrasse
8000 Munich 40
Germany
Tel: (89) 381 6060
Fax: (89) 381 6020

Since 1966, when Ingo Maurer's first lamp was instantly recognized as a design breakthrough, he has won increasing acclaim as a designer and manufacturer of lamps and lighting systems. His work combines elegance and simplicity with unique elements of ironic playfulness and imaginative ingenuity. UK stockists include Catalytico.

Lighting pp. 38, 109

London Lighting Company
135 Fulham Road
London SW3 6RT
England
Tel: (0171) 589 3612
Fax: (0171) 581 9652

Retailers of contemporary designer lighting.

Luceplan SpA
Via E.T. Moneta 56
20161 Milan
Italy
Tel: (02) 66 24 21
Fax: (02) 66 20 34 00

Luceplan was founded at the end of 1979 by architects Riccardo Sarfatti, Sandra Severi and Paolo Rizzatto, after more than fifteen years of experience in the field of lighting. Their initial intention to be the first company in Italy properly equipped to respond to the needs of the contract sector. In 1981 Luceplan won the XII "Compasso d'Oro" design award for the lamp "D7". Luceplan's efforts are directed to realize innovative products which provide a high level of design and, at the same time, are accessible to a wider range of consumers than the designer contract market. UK stockists include Catalytico.

Lighting p. 105

Lucitalia SpA
Via Pelizza de Volpedo 50
20092 Cinisello Balsamo
(MI)
Italy
Tel: (02) 612 6651
Fax: (02) 660 0707

Lighting p. 111

Metalarte SA
Avda. Barcelona 4
08970 Sant Joan Despi
Barcelona
Spain
Tel: (93) 477 0069
Fax: (93) 477 0086

Founded in 1932, Metalarte
in Spain has for more than
half a century developed,
manufactured and marketed
lamps by well-known
designers, takingn the name
into homes worldwide.

Mobles 114 SA
Enric Granados 114
08008 Barcelona
Spain
Tel: (93) 415 78 76
Fax: (93) 237 13 65
Web Site:
www.sidi.es/mobles_114

Manufacturers of modern
furniture and lighting since
1978, Mobles 114 export
products throughout Europe,
Australia, USA, Japan, Hong
Kong and Taiwan, and
participate in projects for
contract business.

Lighting

PAF Srl Nemo/Italiana Luce
c/o Cassina SpA
Via Busnelli 1
20036 Meda (MI)
Italy
Tel: (0362) 340 570
Fax: (03622) 340 559
Web Site: www.cassini.it

Through rigorous and
innovative design and a highly
advanced technological level,
PAF's image has consolidated
worldwide since 1975 when
they began making lights.
Their aim is to bring design to
a wider audience through
serviceable, good-looking,
reasonably priced lights.

SKK Lighting
34 Lexington Street
London W1R 3HR
England
Tel: (0171) 434 4095
Fax: (0171) 287 0168

Contract and domestic lighting
suppliers who also provide
consultation and design
services.

Targetti Sankey
6 Stanton Gate
Mawney Road
Romford
Essex RM7 7HL
England
Tel: (01708) 741 286
Fax: (01708) 742 060

The Targetti group consists
of various companies and
divisions and is the leading
Italian manufacturer of lighting
systems and fixtures. It
operates through its own
facilities, sales offices,
distributors and licensees
throughout the world. The
evolution of lighting technology
has led Targetti to create two
laboratories, one for
computerized photometric
measurements and the other
for testing products to
international safety standards.

Thorn Lighting Ltd
Elstree Way
Borehamwood
Hertfordshire WD6 1HZ
England
Tel: (0181) 905 1313
Fax: (0181) 967 6347
Web Site:
www.thornlight.com

Thorn Lighting is the world's
largest fittings manufacturer
outside the US and Japan,
represented in over 140
countries by subsidiary
companies and agents. The
range includes lighting for
commercial, domestic and
industrial areas, as well as
floodlighting and street
lighting. Developments include
"Sensa" – believed to be the
first truly intelligent fluorescent
fitting for offices.

p. 109

Woka Lamps Vienna Wolfgang Karolinsky
Singerstrasse 16
1010 Wien
Austria
Tel: (222) 5132912
Fax: (222) 5138505

Today, Woka is one of the
authorized manufacturers of
lamps designed by Josef
Hoffmann, Adolf Loos and
other architects from the turn
of the last century in the Woka
Classic Collection, while in the
Art Collection, the aim of
futuristic lighting is to highlight
the year 2000. Woka makes
use of today's creativity to
produce outstanding lighting
designs which meet the
demands of art collectors.

p. 105

Christopher Wray Lighting
199 Shaftsbury Avenue
London WC2H 8JR
England
Tel: (0171) 836 6869
Fax: (0171) 836 6257

Retailers, designers and
manufacturers of lighting.

Storage

Alchimia Trade
Via Cappuccio 14
20123 Milano
Italy

Alchimia in Milan
revolutionizes the way we look
at everyday objects, launching
rounded space capsules to
house televisions and audio
equipment, and reviving
age-old finishes such as water
lacquering, which is hand-
applied and ecologically
sound, for these collector's
items in their "Ollo" collection.

Aram Design
3 Kean Street
Covent Garden
London WC2 4AT
England
Tel: (0171) 240 3933

Retailers and manufacturers
of classic modern furniture.

Arc Linea Arradamenti SpA
Viale Pasubio 50
36030 Caldogno (VI)
Italy
Tel: (0444) 39 41 11
Fax: (0444) 39 42 60
Web Site: www.arclinea.it

Since 1960 Arc Linea in Italy
have made furniture for fitted
kitchens, living rooms and
executive offices, designed
by some of the best Italian
furniture designers: Carlo
Bartoli, Antonio Citterio,
Roberto Pamio.

pp. 128, 130, 133

The Conran Shop Ltd
Shop address:
Michelin House
81 Fulham Road
London SW3 6RD
England
Tel: (0171) 589 7401

Warehouse:
Unit 17
Lee Road
Merton Park Estate
London SW19 3XD
England
Tel: (0171) 589 7401

Retailers of modern designer
furniture and housewares,
including designs by Conran
Collection.

Diseno y Forma SA
63 Rda. Gral. Mitre
08017 Barcelona
Spain

Innovative Spanish furniture
makers commission designs
from international designers.

Shelving

Driade SpA
Via Padana Inferiore 12
(sede)
29012 Fossadello di Caprso
(PC)
Italy
Tel: (0523) 81 86 18
Fax: (0523) 82 23 60

Driade SpA is an Italian
company whose activity in
contemporary design has
been characterized since its
beginning in 1968 by furniture
based on a systemic line of
design, like the storage system
by Antonia Astori, wall-units
"Oikos", kitchen units "Driade
Chef" and office furnishings
"Kaos", and individually
designed pieces of furniture,
grouped as collections.
Marketing activities, through
agents and distributors, covers
most of the worldwide market.

pp. 123, 126, 130, 131

Ecart International
11 rue Saint-Antoine
75004 Paris
France
Tel: (1) 42 78 88 35

Ecart, which spells Trace
backward, develops Andrée
Putman's philosophy of
making progress while
learning from the past. They
market worldwide this French
designer's tableware, furniture,
lights and textiles alongside
classics that come from the
Eileen Gray collection and
Fortuny lighting.

p. 105, 158
*see also Bathrooms, Kitchens
and Lighting*

Enea (Grupo Sidi)
Olla Auzoa 4
20050 Legorreta (Guipuzcoa)
Spain
Tel: (943) 806 275
Fax: (943) 806 374

Enea in Spain make adjustable storage systems, wall to wall, floor to ceiling, in durable but light-weight aluminium, designed for the domestic setting rather than the contract market.

p. 127

Fornasetti Srl
c/o Immaginazione Srl
Via A. Emo
20132 Milan
Italy
Tel: (02) 26 30 60 18
Fax: (02) 25 94 286

Fornasetti Srl has operated in Milan for some years and continues the production of furniture and objects that trompe l'oeil cabinet maker Piero Fornasetti created since the 1950s. His son Barnaba has made new items, sometimes using the same inspirational source. The character of the company is artisanal, and its hand-manufactured products have a limited edition.

p. 27

Inno-Tuote Oy
Merikatu 1
00140 Helsinki
Finland
Tel: (9) 877 0380
Fax: (9) 803 833

Inno has manufactured in Finland architectural interior design products, like furniture, lamps, coat-racks, waste paper baskets, hardware and bathroom accessories since 1975. The general aim is to be "rough but classical", since over-refinement in materials and design becomes banal. High-touch, rather than high-tech is the line on products with personality which will be useful for specifiers in the future.

Interlübke Gebr. Lübke GmbH & Co. KG
Ringstrasse 145
Postfach 1660
D-4840 Rheda-Wiedenbruck
Germany
Tel: (052) 421 21
Fax: (052) 421 2206

With the introduction of its 61-cm-deep "Cupboard Wall" programme 20 years ago, Interlübke upended conventional thinking on how to furnish bedrooms to provide infinitely variable storage systems. They feature standard carcasses which can take hinged, folding or gliding doors, thus coping with every need.

p. 123, 127, 128, 131

I.V.M. SpA
Via C. Cattaneo 90
20035 Lissone (MI)
Italy
Tel: (039) 484315
Fax: (039) 2456815

I.V.M., established in 1950, believes in mass marketing industrialized products. Its home and office furniture and shelving fulfils its philosophy without formalism, based on a design that is more industrial than aesthetic.

Laporta Ltd
The Hop Exchange
24 Southwark Street
London SE1 1TY
England
Tel: (0171) 403 1616
Fax: (0171) 378 0196

UK distributors of Italian office furniture.

Marais International
16 Avenue Victoria
45001 Paris
France
Tel: (1) 42 33 84 84
Fax: (1) 42 36 06 80

Shelving pp. 125, 127

Memphis Srl
Via Olivetti 9
20010 Pregnana Milanese (MI)
Italy
Tel: (02) 9329 0663
Fax: (02) 9329 1202
Web Site:
www.memphis-milano.com

Memphis, the influential cultural furnishing design group, founded in 1981 by Ettore Sottsass, deals with design applied to furnishings. From its beginning, Memphis has overturned and reshaped the presuppositions on which the production of so-called Modern Design is based. Memphis pieces belong in the collections of several museums, and are still manufactured to order.

Shelving

Mobles 114 SA
Enric Granados 114
08008 Barcelona
Spain
Tel: (93) 415 78 76
Fax: (93) 237 13 65
Web Site:
www.sidi.es/mobles_114

Manufacturers of furniture and lighting since 1978, Mobles 114 exports throughout Europe, USA, Australia, Japan, Hong Kong and Taiwan.

see also Lighting p. 177

Muurame Oy
PST Moduli Oy
Pikitie
15560 Nastola
Finland
Tel: (3) 1780 1241
Fax: (3) 1780 5619
Web Site: www.muurame.com

Muurame's production in Finland consists mainly of storage furniture for both home interiors and public areas, marketed through high standard furniture retailers, and exported mainly to the USA, Scandinavia and Belgium.

p. 133

Rexite SpA
Via Edison 7
20090 Cusago (MI)
Italy
Tel: (2) 9016121-5
Fax: (2) 9019954

Rexite SpA, established in 1968 in Cusago, Milan, produces contemporary office and home furnishing fittings, designed by architects Raul Barbieri, Giorgio Marianelli, Giotto Stoppino, Gabriella Montaguti and Kuno Prey. It wins awards on international circuits for its enamelled aluminium storage systems.

Rosenthal Einrichtung
Hindenburgring 9
32339 Espelkamp
Germany
Tel: (5772) 2090
Fax: (5772) 20990
Web Site:
www.einrichtung.rosenthal.de

Rosenthal furniture identifies itself through its functional and aesthetic design, within three themes that mark the bounds of the furniture programme to serve the needs of hospitality; to combine functional design with artistic expression; and to create furniture for living and working. Italian artist Marcello Morandini has created a storage system like a constructivist painting.

pp. 124, 133

Saporiti Italia
Via Gallarete 23
21010 Besnate (VA)
Italy
Tel: (0331) 27 3333
Fax: (331) 273320
Web Site: www.saporitiitalia.it

Saporiti Italia is one of the leading companies in the field of contemporary design and decoration, producing a wide range of models for the decoration of private houses, public spaces, theatres, banks, hotels, restaurants, ships, offices and conference rooms. Since 1945, Sergio and Giorgio Saporiti, with the collaboration of gifted architects, have reached milestones in the history of contemporary furnishings, and shelving systems are one of their concerns in the market.

Sawaya & Moroni
Via Andegari 18
20121 Milan
Italy
Tel: (02) 86 39 51
Fax: (02) 86 46 4831

Founded in 1984 in Milan by interior designers William Sawaya and Paolo Moroni, the company bases its production on contemporary design commissioned from different cultural backgrounds and within different design concepts. This accounts for the individual character and presence of each of their pieces. Production centres on a collection of furniture – divans, tables, chairs, shelves – and a line of small objects, the essential adjuncts to the domestic scene.

Storage p. 132

SCP Ltd
135–139 Curtain Road
London EC2A 3BX
England
Tel: (0171) 739 1869
Fax: (0171) 729 4224

SCP are involved in the revival of Britain's role in the international furniture market, beginning in 1980 by dealing in classic 1930s originals, then expanding to commission designs from Matthew Hilton, Jasper Morrison and Nigel Coates. SCP's policy is to work with a small number of designers on a long-term basis.

Shelving

Tecta
Sohnreystrasse 10
3471 Lauenfoerde
Germany
Tel: (5273) 7006
Fax: (5273) 8410

Tecta produces the classics of the Bauhaus movement together with contemporary furniture like the storage systems and kitchen "tree" by Stefan Wewerka.

p. 126

Tonelli Srl
Via della Produzione 61
61025 Montelabate (PS)
Italy
Tel: (0721) 481339
Fax: (0721) 481291

p. 124, 125

J. Tressera Design SL
c/ Josep Bertrand
08021 Barcelona
Spain
Tel: (93) 2004922
Fax: (93) 2004734
Web Site:
www.global.com.es/tressera

Tressera designed fitted sets in the movie "Batman". They regularly win international awards for their design and quality of cabinetry. The materials used are, essentially, walnut veneer, finished with various light- and dark- toned varnishes, blended with inlaid marquetry which perfects the finish and brings out the quality of the furniture.

Screens p. 27, 133
see also Walls & Ceilings, p. 169

Wallace Brown Ltd
71 Marionville Road
Edinburgh EH7 6AH
Scotland
Tel: (0131) 661 9962
Fax: (0131) 652 0956

An office furniture retailer, which also offers its customers interior design and planning for home and office.

Zerodisegno-Quattrocchio Srl
Via Isonzo 51
15100 Alessandria
Italy
Tel: (0131) 445 361
Fax: (0131) 68745
Web Site: www.zerodisegno.it

A bicycle manufacturer, Quattrocchio, which was established in Italy in 1919, turned to modular shop fittings for storage, and then introduced a collection of complementary pieces of free-standing storage systems.

Bathrooms

Agape Srl
Via Ploner 2
46038 Frassino (MA)
Italy
Tel: (0376) 3713839
Fax: (0376) 3742137

Since 1973 Agape have produced and distributed bathroom furnishings. A characteristic of their product is the design and the precision of finishes on wash basins and bathroom accessories like mirrors with built-in halogen light and dimmers.

pp. 147, 150
see also Kitchens, p. 181

Albatros System SpA
Via Valcellina
Zona Industriale Nord
33097 Spilimbergo (PN)
Italy

Tel: (0427) 59 41 11
Fax: (0427) 50 304

Albatros System has developed the bathroom concept with its advanced technology of hydromassage tubs. Safe and reliable systems applied to ergonomic bathtubs in various forms and colours are leading to a larger share of the market. Applications include injection systems at the base of a minipool, refinements like underwater light, and hydromassage heads.

Hot tubs

American Standard
PO Box 6820
Piscataway NJ 08855
USA
Tel: (908) 980 3326

Fittings

Aqualisa Products Ltd
The Flyer's Way
Westerham
Kent TN16 1DE
England
Tel (01959) 63240

Showers

Barking Water Technology Ltd
1 River Road
Barking
Essex IG11 0HD
England
Tel: (0181) 594 7292
Fax: (0181) 594 8898
Web Site: www.grohe.co.uk

p. 168

Barovier & Toso Vetrerie Art. Riunite Srl
Fondamenta Vetrai 28
30141 Murano (VE)
Italy
Tel: (041) 739049
Fax: (041) 737385

p. 150

Brovedan Brothers Import Services
181 Kensington Road
London SE11 6ST
England
Tel: (0171) 735 6063

UK distributors of Italian bathroom fittings.

Carrara & Matta SpA
Via O. Vigliani 24
10135 Turin
Italy
Tel: (011) 343444
Fax: (011) 343859

Established in 1940, Carrara & Matta SpA is a leading manufacturer of plastic bathroom accessories, bathroom furniture, seats and shower curtains and rails. Top quality and design have always been the guidelines of Carrara & Matta policy.

Bathroom accessories p. 150

Cesame SpA
Zona Industriale
95100 Catania
Italy
Tel: (095) 591044
Fax: (095) 592613

Among the first bathroom fittings manufacturers to convert the production of fireclay to a porcelained fine gres – using British kaolin and clay – comparable to porcelain. Cesame markets worldwide two ranges: the one exploiting craft fascination of the ceramic art, the other since 1966 promoting enamelling.

Fittings

Cesana SpA
Via Dalmazia 3
20059 Vimercate
Italy
Tel: (039) 60 82 441
Fax: (039) 66 11 66

From what was initially a family mirror and glassware business in 1965 to the four plants which now create over 5,000 different solutions for glass shower stalls, Cesana has achieved a production record in bathroom fittings. They introduced the system of plumbing within a single pillar in which the activating mixing valve is located.

Fittings p. 144

Czech and Speake
39 Jermyn Street
London SW1Y 6DN
England
Tel: (0171) 439 0216
Fax: (0171) 734 8587

Famous bathroom fittings manufacturers with a big range of Edwardian mixer taps are enjoying a revival in modern interiors such as John Young's Thamesreach Penthouse in London.

Bathrooms pp. 135, 137

Daryl Industries Ltd
Alfred Road
Wallasey
Wirral L44 7HY
England
Tel: (0151) 606 5000
Fax: (0151) 638 0300

Since 1967, Daryl have been developing a reputation for innovation and quality in bathroom fixtures, introducing features that are industry standards today. Daryl anodize the aluminium frames for shower doors, enclosures and bath screens, using only toughened safety glass suitable for power showers and steam systems. Their adjustable wall sections mean that each unit fits precisely on walls that are not perfectly vertical. All screens are reversible for left and right installation, and are fully assembled for easy installation. You can choose from the full range of frame finishes and glazing options which are described in the Daryl Price Book that accompanies their brochure.

Corner showers pp. 140, 145

Aloys F. Dornbracht GmbH & Co. KG
Postfach 1454
Koebbingser Muehle 6
5860 Iserlohn
Germany
Tel: (2371) 4330
Fax: (2371) 433232
Web Site: www.dornbracht.com

Dornbracht is well-known worldwide for its design-oriented plumbing products. Dornbracht incorporates unique European design with quality German craftsmanship, precision and engineering to produce these bath fittings. For over half a century, Dornbracht has established world standards for decorative brass bath fittings.

Bathroom taps pp. 136, 137, 148, 149

Duravit AG
Werderstrasse 36
Postfach 240
7746 Hornberg
Germany
Tel: (78)33 700
Fax: (78)33 70289
Web Site: www.duravit.ag

Founded in 1817 as an earthenware factory in the Black Forest, Duravit today present the "Dellarco" designer series in bathroom fixtures from sanitary ceramics to bathroom accessories. The third largest manufacturer of bathroom ceramic products, Duravit combine the ancient skill of pottery with the demands of full-scale factory production.

Fittings pp. 123, 139, 147

Ecart International
11 rue Saint-Antoine
75004 Paris
France
Tel: (1) 42 78 88 35

Ecart, which spells Trace backward, develops Andrée Putman's philosophy of making progress while learning from the past. They market worldwide this French designer's tableware, furniture, lights and textiles alongside classics from the Eileen Gray collection and Fortuny lighting.

p. 105, 158
see also Kitchens and Lighting

F.I.R. Rubinetterie SpA
Strada Statale
28010 Vaprio d'Agnona
Italy
Tel: (0321) 99 62 21
Fax: (0321) 99 64 26

Established in the late 1950s, FIR Rubinetterie produce traditional taps and valves mainly for worldwide export from Italy. From 1970, the commercial and production trend changed completely, and FIR concentrated on creating "top quality, designed and coloured taps", and studied technical solutions to ensure the greatest efficiency and longest durability.

Bathroom taps

Frascio SpA
Via Nazionale 6
25070 Agnosine (BS)
Italy
Tel: (0365) 866385
Fax: (0365) 866102
Web Site: www.frascio.com

Through research carried out in collaboration with designers, ideas for bath fittings at Frascio take shape on paper, then solidly in steel moulds, an exciting transition in the process of creativity. The balance between machine moulding and manual work within the factory give the pieces a tactile and friendly quality. Frascio has operated since 1945 as a family business.

Accessories

GEC Anderson Ltd
89 Hurkomer Road
Bushey
Hertfordshire WD2 3LS
England
Tel: (0181) 950 1826
Fax: (0181) 950 3626

Stainless steel sanitary ware used in the Thamesreach Penthouse of John Young.

Bathrooms pp. 135, 137

Gruppo Novellini
Via della Stazione 2
46030 Romanore Borgoforte (MN)
Italy
Tel: (0376) 64911
Fax: (0376) 648267

Combining Italian design with European quality requirements, Novellini is a leading Italian manufacturer of shower screens in laminated safety glass, and acrylic whirlpools.

UK outlet:
Novellini Bathroom Products
Unit 5H
Tewkesbury Industrial Centre
Delta Drive
Tewkesbury
Gloucestershire GL20 8HD
England
Tel: (01684) 297570
Fax: (01684) 850912

Handles and Fittings Ltd
HAF House
Mead Lane
Hertford
Hertfordshire SG13 7AP
England
Tel: (01922) 505 655
Fax: (01922) 505 705
Web Site:
www.giant.co.uk.hafl.htm

Specialists in architectural
ironmongery, Handles and
Fittings Ltd introduced three
ranges of contemporary door
furniture which was extended
to encompass bathroom
accessories, electrical fittings,
door closers and locks, all
made exclusively for them
in England.

Inno-Tuote Oy
Merikatu 1
00140 Helsinki
Finland
Tel: (9) 877 0380
Fax: (9) 877 03833

Inno has manufactured in
Finland architectural interior
design products, like furniture,
lamps, coat-racks, waste
paper baskets, hardware and
bathroom accessories since
1975. The general aim is to be
"rough but classical", since
over-refinement in materials
and design becomes banal.
High-touch, rather than high-
tech is the line on products
with personality which will
be useful for specifiers in
the future.

see also Storage p. 178

Kartell SpA
Via delle Industrie 1
20082 Noviglio (MI)
Italy
Tel: (02) 900 121
Fax: (02) 900 91212
Web Site: www.kartell.it

Kartell, founded in the 1950s,
is today a leader in the
production of plastic
furnishings, distinguished from
others by collaboration with
some of the most famous
international designers,
including Matteo Thun's
mirror collection.

Mirrors p. 150

M & Z
Via Casale 37
28010 Bolzano Novarese
(NO)
Italy
Tel: (0322) 982086
Fax: (0322) 982226

Manufacturer of sanitary
fittings with 20 years
experience, Rubinetteria
M & Z makes bath and
kitchen taps in different
colours and finishes by
world famous designers.

Bathroom taps p. 149

Majestic Shower Company
1 North Place
Edinburgh Way
Harlow
Essex CM20 2SL
England
Tel: (01279) 443644
Fax: (01279) 635074
Web Site:
www.majesticshowers.com

Fittings

Milldue Arredi SpA
Via Balegante 7
31039 Riese Pio X (TV)
Italy
Tel: (0423) 485041-2
Fax (0423) 456319

Milldue, specialists in the
production of bathroom
furniture, was founded in
1977. From the start, its aim
was to market top designs,
while not forgetting the final
cost to the customer, in
walnut, polyester, lacquer
and maple, with worktops
supplied in polyester lacquer,
marble or granite.

Fittings

Nordic Saunas Ltd
Fairview Estate
Holland Road
Oxted
Surrey RH8 9BZ
England
Tel: (01883) 732 400
Fax: (01883) 716 970

Firm specializing in saunas,
showers and bathroom fittings.

Oespag Laufen AG
Goethegasse 3
1015 Vienna
Austria
Tel: (222) 51597-0
Fax (222) 51597222

Laufen is one of Europe's
leading ceramic
manufacturers, with factories
located all over the world.
Throughout all Laufen's
various design and
manufacturing divisions,
which include production of
bathroom fixtures, wall and
floor tiles, tableware, chimney
stacks, insulators and roof
tiles, the company's
philosophy is quality, design
and functionality. Their latest
washbasin, water closet,
hand-basin and bidet, all
designed by F.A. Porsche,
operate as a furnishing
scheme rather than separate
fittings, unified within a base
cabinet, allowing combinations
of components on a modular
system.

Fittings p. 145

Pegler Ltd
St Catherine's Avenue
Doncaster
South Yorkshire DN4 8DF
England
Tel: (01302) 368 581
Fax: (01302) 367 661

Manufacturers of bathroom
fittings and accessories.

Ponsi Rubinetterie Toscane
Via A. Volta 2
55049 Viareggio (LU)
Italy
Tel: (0584) 46132
Fax (0584) 64117
Web Site: www.ponsi.it

Since 1935, Ponsi have
designed and manufactured
taps and bathroom
accessories. Production is
carried out in Tuscany, from
the foundry to despatch and
sales. The greatest care is
taken in aesthetics, quality
and reliability.

Preedy Glass
7B Coronation Road
London NW0 7PQ
England
Tel: (0181) 965 1323

Established in London for
more than 75 years, the family
glass firm J. Preedy & Sons
provides comprehensive
services to the architectural,
interior design and household
markets. They are also UK
distributors for French
manufactured quality
architectural fixtures and
fittings from Stremler and
Adler, including glass doors,
panels and shower
enclosures.

Bathroom accessories

Rapsel SpA
Via Volta 13
20019 Settimo Milanese
(MI)
Italy
Tel: (02) 33 50 141

In the 1970s, Rapsel began
marketing first textiles, then
bath fittings from Scandinavia,
with Vola taps. Then they
commissioned designs for
baths and basins stylish
enough for the streamlined
taps, producing the
"washmobil" by Berger and
Stahl, then "Euclide" by Finn
Skoedt, then Philippe Starck's
basin in 1985, "Rapsody" by
Berger and Stahl and in 1990
"Pan" by Tun and Gagliardi.

Fittings pp. 147, 150

Rubinetterie Teorema SpA
Via XX Settembre 120
25020 Flero (BS)
Italy
Tel: (30) 3580791
Fax: (30) 2680645

Teorema, based in Northern
Italy in an area with a
reputation since medieval
times for metalworking,
reconciles this historical
tradition with Italian
contemporary design for their
series of taps.

Bathroom taps pp. 148, 149

Schmidt-Lackner-Design
Marktplatz 2
6900 Heidelberg
Germany
Tel: (6221) 163280
Fax: (6221) 163780

The formal bathroom moves
on with playful, yet functional
accessories, like handles and
rings that clip on to change
the colour trims on taps with
Schmidt-Lackner's plastic
fittings.

Taps p. 149
see also Kitchens, p. 182

Stelrad Bathroom Products Ltd
PO Box 103
National Avenue
Hull HU5 4JN
England
Tel: (01482) 492 251
Fax: (01482) 448 858
Web Site: www.caradon.com

Fittings

StudioLine Collections Srl
Via F.lli Rossellini 17/18
Fontane die Villorba Z1 (TV)
Italy
Tel: (0422) 60 80 44
Fax: (0422) 60 81 66

StudioLine's range of
complementary accessories in
many materials from ceramics
and metal to wood and marble
allows a choice of fittings and
fixtures in the bathroom to
provide the best use of
available space.

Fittings p. 150

Svedbergs of Sweden Ltd
717 Fulham Road
London SW6 5UL
England
Tel: (0171) 371 9214
Fax: (0171) 371 8266

Market leader in Scandinavia,
Svedbergs bathrooms offer the
complete package from baths,
showers, basins and lavatories
to specialist fittings like
whirlpool baths and vanity
units, as well as ceiling tiles
with built-in stereo
loudspeakers and
halogen lights.

p. 28

Tantofex Ltd
Birches Industrial Estate
Imberhorne Lane
East Grinstead
West Sussex RH19 1XG
England
Tel: (01342) 328 166
Fax: (01342) 410 353

Toni Armatur A/S
Rodovre
Denmark
Tel: (361) 01422

Bathroom taps p. 149

Toscoquattro Srl
Via P. Calamandrei sn
51031 Agliana (PT)
Italy
Tel: (0574) 751289
Fax: (0574) 712005

Toscoquattro products range
from bathroom cabinets in
solid wood with marble tops to
bathroom accessories. Careful
choice of materials and
interesting designs have built
up their sales reputation in
Japan, Canada and Europe
since their launch in 1980.

Fittings

Vola UK
Venus Bath Centre
Unit 12
Ampthill Business Park
Station Road
Ampthill
Bedfordshire MK45 2QW
England
Tel: (01525) 841 155
Fax: (01525) 841 177

UK outlet for the Vola range
of kitchen and bathroom
fittings manufactured by the
Danish firm I.P. Lund.

Taps p. 148
see also Kitchens, p.183

The Water Monopoly
16 Lonsdale Road
London NW6
England
Tel: (0171) 624 2636
Fax: (0171) 624 2631

Fittings

Kitchens

AEG (UK) Ltd
Cornwall House
55–57 High Street
Slough
Berkshire SL1 1DZ
England
Tel: (01753) 872 438
Fax: (01753) 872 411
Web Site:
www.aeghausgeraete.de

AEG stands for Advanced
Engineering from Germany
and since the end of the last
century AEG have applied the
latest technology to develop
domestic appliances for
cooking, dish- or clothes-
washing and drying,
refrigeration, vacuum cleaning
and ventilation. The company
is dedicated to ecological
saving of energy and water
and began, in 1979, a
manufacturing policy
dedicated to "caring for
the environment through
technology".

Appliances

Agape Srl
Via Ploner 2
46038 Frassino (MA)
Italy
Tel: (0376) 3713839
Fax: (0376) 3742137

Since 1973 Agape have
produced and distributed
elements to furnish the
bathroom. A characteristic of
their product is the design and
the precision of finishes on
wash basins and bathroom
accessories like mirrors with
built-in halogen light and
dimmers.

pp. 147, 150

Allmilmo-Milewski Moebelwerk Zeil KG
97470 Zeil am Main
Germany
Tel: (9524) 910
Fax: (9524) 9925

p. 158

Alno AG
88629 Pfullendorf
Germany
Tel: 07552-21-0
Fax: 07552-213400
Web Site: www.alno.de

Since 1930, Alno have made
kitchens, in wood – solid
oak or modern laminate
combinations – or with a
high gloss finish in a wide-
ranging programme from
traditional fronts and detailing
to stream-lined modernity.
The largest independent
kitchen manufacturer in
Europe, Alno give priority
to recyclable materials and
renewable resources, using
only local wood.

pp. 153, 159, 160

UK outlet:
Alno (UK) Ltd
Unit 10
Hampton Farm Industrial
Estate
Hampton Road West
Hanworth
Middlesex TW13 6DB
England
Tel: (0181) 898 4781
Fax: (0181) 898 0268

ATAG (UK) Ltd
19–20 Hither Green
Clevedon
Somerset BS21 6XU
England
Tel: (01275) 877 301
Fax: (01275) 871 371

UK outlet for the Dutch
kitchen appliance
manufacturer ATAG
Keukentechniek.

Avonite
Sylmar Technology Ltd
10 Alderman's Hill
Palmers Green
London N13 4PJ
England
Tel: (0181) 447 8090
Fax: (0181) 882 9887
Web Site: www.avonite.com

pp. 166, 167

Boffi SpA
Via Oberdan 70
20030 Lentate sul Seveso
(MI)
Italy
Tel: (0362) 562881
Fax: (0362) 565077
Web Site: www.boffi.it

Boffi Arredamento Cucina are
known worldwide for their
kitchen design. Since 1940,
Italian Boffi have launched
some innovations: the first
coloured polyester door finish,
the first door without a handle
grip, and also the first door
with vertical wood strips.

pp. 161, 164

Robert Bosch Domestic Appliances Ltd
Grand Union House
Old Wolverton Road
Wolverton
Milton Keynes
Buckinghamshire MK12 5PT
England
Tel: (01908) 328 262
Fax: (01908) 328 560

p. 163

Bulthaup GmbH & Co
84153 Aich
Germany
Tel: (8741) 80274
Fax: (8741) 80309
Web Site: www.bulthaup.com

The name Bulthaup is well-
known internationally for top
design and innovative
technology in kitchens, and
has received many awards.
Nearly 150 different colours
and a wide variety of wood
and laminate finishes are
used. Bulthaup showrooms
are to be found in every
major European city.

Storage pp. 154, 165

UK outlet:
Bulthaup Furniture Systems
The Kitchen People Ltd
37 Wigmore Street
London W1H 9LD
England
Tel: (0171) 495 3663
Fax: (0171) 495 0139

Ciatti SpA
Via del Botteghino-fraz.badia
A Set
50010 Scandicci (FI)
Italy
Tel: (055) 73 10 817
Fax: (055) 73 10 827

Ciatti, a leading manufacturer
of top-grade, complementary
kitchen furniture, is renowned
for innovative design and
versatility. Italian country
pieces reinterpreted in light
and airy beech, like the sturdy
but elegant chairs and stools,
accent the revolutionary Axis
free-standing system for the
smaller kitchen.

Effeti SpA
Via B. Cellini 174
50028 Tavarnelle V.P. (FI)
Italy
Tel: (055) 8070007-9
Fax: (055) 8070085
Web Site: www.effiti.com

Guaranteed by a solid in-house
production in the finest tradition
of Tuscan carpentry, the
Effeti kitchen brings vigour to
inspired design and innovative
styling, like trimming the
corner with curvacious units
fitted with specially curved
cooking appliances.

Appliances p. 156

F.lli Ferretti de Ferretto SpA
Via Volterrana 60
56003 Capannoli (PI)
Italy
Tel: (050) 587 63 91 11
Fax: (050) 587 60 91 46

Fittings pp. 157, 162, 167

Foster Beard Ltd
Oxgate Lane
Cricklewood
London NW2 7JN
England
Tel: (0181) 452 3399
Fax: (0800) 22846

Durability, practicality and
good looks combine to make
the "Blancostone" sink a major
innovation in the kitchen. Made
from Siligranit, a composite
material of 80% natural granite
and 20% acrylic, Blancostone
offers a smooth, hard-wearing,
easy-to-clean work surface to
complement today's high-
quality fitted kitchens.

Sinks

Franke UK Ltd
East Park
Manchester
International Office Centre
Styal Road
Manchester M22 5WB
England
Tel: (0161) 436 6280
Fax: (0161) 436 2180
Web Site: www.franke.ch

The world's leading sink
manufacturers, Franke from
Switzerland produce sinks,
taps, hobs and waste
disposers that are widely
available through kitchen
specialists, quality builders'
and plumbers' merchants,
departmental stores and
home centres.

Sinks

Grey & Co
Fyning Copse
Rogate
Petersfield
Hampshire GU31 5DH
England
Tel: (01730) 821 424
Fax: (01730) 821 717
Web Site:
www.johnnygrey.co.uk

Johnny Grey has worked for
20 years in the kitchen
business and developed the
concept of the "Unfitted
Kitchen" based on the
traditional farmhouse kitchen
adapted to contemporary
needs and to fit modern
appliances.

I.P. Lund Trading APS
Axel Kiers Vej 12
8270 Højbjerg
Denmark
Tel: (8629) 1444
Fax: (8629) 2459

Vola taps, made in Denmark,
are a hallmark of architectural
design, the spout simplified to
simulate a stream of water.
The unique combination of
designer skills and fine
handicraft became reality with
the introduction of the Vola
design created in 1968 by one
of the leading architect/
designers of the 20th century,
Arne Jacobsen. Today Vola is
installed throughout the world.
They are represented in the
UK by Vola UK.

Kitchen taps p. 168
see also Bathrooms, p. 182

Magnificent Marble
High Street
Sutton
Surrey
England
Tel: (0181) 643 1723

Magnificent Marble
manufactures fireplaces and
hearths, kitchen worktops,
and bathroom vanity tops and
both bath and wall panels in
marble and granite at their
workshop and showroom in
Surrey. The company which
began in 1989 offers a design,
manufacturing and fitting
stonemasonry service to
interior designers.

Fireplaces

Merloni Domestic Appliances Ltd
Merloni House
3 Cowley Business Park
Cowley
Uxbridge
Middlesex UB8 2AD
England
Tel: (01895) 858 208
Fax: (01322) 234 695

Merloni has two brands,
Ariston and Indesit; Indesit the
reliable, but affordable brand,
and Ariston, the innovative
and sophisticated.

Appliances p. 163

Miele Company Ltd
Fairacres
Marcham Road
Abingdon
Oxon OX14 1TW
England
Tel: (01235) 554455
Fax: (01235) 554477
Web Site: www.miele.de

Miele began making
appliances known as the Rolls
Royce of the home help
range, and then began
production in the 1970s of
cabinets and fittings to house
them. Now, the name Miele is
synonymous with quality
kitchens throughout the world.
Their design and production
technology combined in a
wide range of stylish kitchens
in wood, laminate, lacquer
and high gloss finishes, offers
the architect a service
covering design, costing and
installation.

pp. 154, 155, 163

Neff UK Ltd
Grand Union House
Old Wolverton Road
Wolverton
Milton Keynes
Buckinghamshire MK12 5PT
England
Tel: (01908) 328 300
Fax: (01908) 328 560
Web Site:
www.neff-online.com

Appliances pp. 162, 163, 165

Pegler Ltd
St Catherine's Avenue
Doncaster
South Yorkshire DN4 8DF
England
Tel: (01302) 368 581
Fax: (01302) 367 661

Taps p. 168

Philips Whirlpool (UK) Ltd
PO Box 45
City House
420/430 London Road
Croydon
Surrey CR9 2ZX
England
Tel: (0181) 689 2166
Fax: (0181) 689 9179

pp. 162, 164

Poggenpohl GmbH & Co
Herringhauser Str. 33
Postfach 2455
D-4900 Herford
Germany
Tel: (05221) 3810
Fax: (05221) 381321

For almost one hundred years Poggenpohl have manufactured kitchens in Herford. Although many changes have occurred in the production processes, one objective has remained the same: the high-quality and precision of their custom-built kitchens together with contemporary design and highest functionality. Over many decades and in over 40 countries worldwide Poggenpohl has gained a high reputation, thus creating a prestigious world-class name.

pp. 155, 156, 157, 160, 161, 162

UK outlet:
Poggenpohl Group UK Ltd
2nd Floor
Silbury Court
368 Silbury Boulevard
Milton Keynes MK9 2AF
England
Tel: (01908) 606 886
Fax: (01908) 606 958

Robert Bosch Hausgeraete GmbH
Postfach 10 60 50
70049 Stuttgart
Germany
Tel: (711) 8110
Fax: (711) 811 6630

Represented around the world, Robert Bosch prides itself in kitchen design that employs the latest technology, elegantly clad in a wide variety of door fronts, cabinet types and finishes to make an individual kitchen that lines up with their extensive range of dishwashers, as well as refrigeration, cooking and home laundry appliances.

UK outlet:
Robert Bosch Domestic Appliances Ltd
Grand Union House
Old Wolverton Road
Wolverton
Milton Keynes
Buckinghamshire MK12 5PT
England
Tel: (01908) 328 262
Fax: (01908) 328 560

Salima/Tecnoarredo Srl
Via Mazzini 154
Chiusi Scalo (FI)
Italy
Tel: (0578) 20350
Fax: (0578) 227459

The aim of the Salima factory is to find a high-quality market. Able to satisfy customers' requests when they do not want a mass-produced article, Salima only needs three days to custom-build particular designs. At their permanent exhibition-standard kitchen, designs are open for viewing.

Storage p. 160, 165

Scavolini SpA
Via Risara 60/70
61025 Montelabbate (PS)
Italy
Tel: (0721) 4431
Fax: (0721) 482336
Web Site: www.scavolini.com

Scavolini, a leading Italian kitchen producer, distributes worldwide with increasing success; its warm and rational kitchens represent the best of Italian design. Accurate targeting and marketing of Scavolini assures the best service possible to customers.

p. 156

Schmidt-Lackner-Design
Marktplatz 2
6900 Heidelberg
Germany
Tel: (6221) 163 280
Fax: (6221) 163 780

The formal bathroom moves on with playful, yet functional accessories, such as handles and rings that clip on to change the colour of the trims on taps with Schmidt-Lackner's plastic fittings.

Kitchen taps p. 149
see also Bathrooms p. 181

Siematic Möbelwerke GmbH & Co
August-Siekmann Str. 1–5
32582 Löhne
Germany
Tel: (5732) 670
Fax: (5732) 67 297
Web Site: www.siematic.de

Siematic, designers and builders of kitchens since 1930, are responsible for many innovations under the watchful eye of the founder's heir August Siekmann. Distributed throughout Europe and the USA, their 34 ranges offer high-gloss lacquer finishes, combined with polished chrome or brass fittings, and strong colour (they have introduced brilliant red to their 2002G, 400RG and 9009PR ranges).

pp. 155, 157, 161, 167

UK outlet:
Siematic UK Ltd
11/17 Fowler Road
Hainault Industrial Estate
Ilford
Essex IG6 3UU
England
Tel: (0181) 500 1944
Fax: (0181) 500 9102
Web Site:
www.siematic.co.uk

Siemens Domestic Appliances Ltd
Grand Union House
Old Wolverton Road
Wolverton
Milton Keynes
Buckinghamshire MK12 5PT
England
Tel: (01908) 328 400
Fax: (01908) 328 499
Web Site: www.siemens.de

p. 162

Smallbone & Co (Devizes) Ltd
Hopton Industrial Estate
London Road
Devizes
Wiltshire SN10 2EU
England
Tel: (01380) 729090

Shop:
105–109 Fulham Road
London SW3 6RL
Tel: (0171) 581 9989

Smallbone of Devizes are a leading kitchen design company in the UK, offering a range of custom-built kitchens, hand-made in their workshop in Wiltshire. They were the first company to introduce reclaimed pine, to revive bleached and limed wood finishes and introduce contemporary unfitted kitchens with hand-painted techniques on kitchen furniture.

Smeg SpA
Via Circonvallazione Nord 26
42016 Guastalla (RE)
Italy
Tel: (0522) 83 77 77
Fax: (0522) 83 83 84
Web Site: www.smeg.it

From the first automatic gas cookers to the latest electronic built-in ovens, the development of electrical household appliances over the last 35 years by Smeg SpA of Guastalla, Italy, has brought the company to the forefront in the built-in oven sector in both Italy and the world. From the 1970s, the company has been developing a policy of innovation in all sectors of electrical household goods, putting a series of appliances, both built-in and free-standing, onto the market, that are not just technologically perfect, but also well designed and attractive.

p. 165

UK outlet:
Smeg (UK) Ltd
Corinthian Court
80 Milton Park
Abingdon
Oxon OX14 4RY
England
Tel: (01235) 828 315
Fax: (01235) 821 120

Strato SnC
Via Piemonte 9
23018 Talamona (SO)
Italy
Tel: (0342) 358 116
Fax: (0342) 358 525

Strato was created in 1987 by Marco Gorini & Gianna Farina.

pp. 153, 155, 161

Sylmar Technology Ltd
See Avonite

Tantofex Ltd
Birches Industrial Estate
Imberhorne Lane
East Grinstead
West Sussex RH19 1XG
England
Tel: (01342) 328 166
Fax: (01342) 410 353

Taps p. 168

Tielsa
Postfach 362045
4902 Bad Salzuflen
Germany
Tel: (5223) 165-0
Fax: (5223) 165111

Part of Wellmann GmbH, Europe's largest rigid kitchen manufacturer, Tielsa are renowned for their innovative use of unusual materials, in 73 kitchen designs with matching cabinets in laminates, lacquers, oaks, pines and maple, aimed at the top end of the market.

Villeroy and Boch AG
Reifster 46
66663 Merzig
Germany
Tel: (68) 64 811
Fax: (68) 64 81405

Villeroy & Boch, manufacturers of fine ceramics for 250 years, introduced a range of efficient kitchen sinks, combining modern design with superior quality in ceramic or the new synthetic materials. Villeroy & Boch's kitchen sinks are curved and organic; octagonal, which can be fitted across corners; rounded or squared, in a wide choice of sizes.

Sinks pp. 166, 168

Woodstock Furniture Limited
4 William Street
London SW1X 9HL
England
Tel: (0171) 837 1818
Fax: (0171) 837 1852

Working principally in
hardwoods (from sustainable
sources) Woodstock's
cabinetmakers build each
cabinet from scratch, usually a
combination of fitted and
unfitted pieces.

Cabinets

Zanussi Elettrodomestici SpA
Marketing Rex
Corso Lino Zanussi 30
Porcia (PO)
Italy
Tel: (0434) 39 55 58
Fax: (0434) 39 60 46
Web Site: www.zanussi.com

Zanussi, belonging to the
Electrolux Group, is the
leading manufacturing
company in Europe for "white
goods". The Zanussi brand is
well-known and established in
all the European countries.
Design and innovation are the
basic tools of a strategy aimed
to satisfy the emerging needs
of European consumers. The
"Wizard" collection of white
goods styled and finished in
matte-black won them
international awards.

Appliances pp. 152, 164

UK outlet:
Zanussi Ltd
55–57 High Street
Slough
Berkshire SL1 1DZ
England
Tel: (01753) 872 348
Fax: (01753) 872 411

Zerowatt SpA
Via Busa 19
24020 Alzano Lombardo
(BG)
Italy
Tel: (035) 47 91 11
Fax: (035) 513251
Web Site: www.candy.it

The best-known products
of Zerowatt are washing-
machines, washer-dryers, and
dryers. Space-saving is their
aim. Zerowatt has integrated
the high technology of a 5 kg/
front-loading washing machine
in a slim-line appliance with a
depth of only 17 in (42 cm).
This saves about 30% in
space compared to a standard
washing-machine for 5kg. In
1989, Zerowatt launched the
"Spaziozero 33" washing-
machine, only 13in (33cm)
in depth. Another famous
product of Zerowatt is "1007
Electronic", the only appliance
which can wash and dry
automatically 4kg of laundry,
compared with the 2kg or
2.5kg which can be done by
any other washer-dryer.

Miscellaneous

The Building Centre
26 Store Street
London WC1E 7BT
England
Tel: (0171) 637 1022

The Design Council
28 Haymarket Street
London SW14 4SU
England
Tel: (0171) 839 8000

Italian Trade Centre
Government Agency
37 Sackville Street
London W1X 2DQ
England
Tel: (0171) 734 2412/8

Government-sponsored
agency promotes
manufactured Italian products
for the building trade and
furnishing at home.

Architects and Designers

Tadao Ando Architect and Associates
5–23 Toyosaki 2
Chome Osadu-Ku
Osaka
Japan 531
Tel: (6) 375 1148

Architecture

Ron Arad Associates
62 Chalk Farm Road
London NW1 8AN
England
Tel: (0171) 284 4965

Design

Aukett Associates
2 Great Eastern Wharf
Parkgate Road
London SW11 4TT
England
Tel: (0171) 924 4949
Fax: (0171) 924 6720

Architecture

Albert Bardawil
6–28 Hyde Park Gardens
London W2 2NB
England
Tel: (0171) 262 6415
Fax: (0171) 402 2855

Architecture

Ottorino & Cecilia Berselli
Via Luzzago 6
25100 Brescia
Italy
Tel: (030) 37 74 139
Fax: (030) 24 20 886

Architecture

Gianfranco Cavaglia Architect
Via Giolitti N. 11
10123 Turin
Italy
Tel: (011) 54 81 68
Fax: (011) 56 22 228

Architecture

Chassay & Last Architects
Berkeley Works
Berkeley Road
London NW1 8XY
England
Tel: (0171) 402 3233
Fax: (0171) 262 1475

Architecture

David Chipperfield Associates
1a Cobham Mews
Agar Grove
London NW1 9SB
England
Tel: (0171) 267 9422
Fax: (0171) 267 9347

Architecture

David Connor International
10 Ivebury Court
325 Latimer Road
London W10 6RA
England
Tel: (0181) 964 5357
Fax: (0181) 964 5679

Architecture

Cunningham Architects
4136 Commerce Street #200
Dallas
TX 75201
USA
Tel: (214) 821 9525
Fax: (214) 821 9526

Architecture

Lynn Davis Architects
Gazen Salts Studios
Rear of Guestling Mill
Strand Street
Sandwich
Kent CT13 9HN
England
Tel: (01304) 612 089
Fax: (01304) 620 675

Architecture

**DIN Associates Ltd Design
Consultants**
32 St Oswald's Place
London SE11 5JE
England
Tel: (0171) 582 0777

Architecture/Design

Epton Studio
Via Cernaia 1
10121 Turin
Italy
Tel: (011) 61 39 15
Fax: (011) 61 38 17

Architecture

Frank Fitzgibbons
4822 Glencairn Road
Los Angeles CA 90027
USA
Tel: (323) 663 7579
Fax: (323) 663 6262

Architecture

Steven Forman Architect
160 East 48th Street
Studio 12-0
New York, NY 10017
USA
Tel: (212) 486 0352
Fax: (212) 472 5631

Architecture

Future Systems
See Jan Kaplicky

Alexander Gorlin
137 Varick
New York NY 10013
USA
Tel: (212) 229 1199
Fax: (212) 206 3590

Architecture

Michael Graves
241 Nassau Street
Princeton NJ 08450
USA
Tel: (609) 924 6409
Fax: (609) 924 1795

Architecture

Gwathmey Siegel & Associates
475 Tenth Avenue
New York NY 10018
USA
Tel: (212) 947 1240
Fax: (212) 967 0890
Web Site:
www.gwathmey-siegel.com

Architecture

Steven Holls Architects
435 Hudson Street
New York
NY 10014
USA
Tel: (212) 989 0918
Fax: (212) 463 9718
Web Site:
www.stevenholl.com

Architecture

Michael Hopkins & Partners
27 Broadley Terrace
London NW1 6LG
England
Tel: (0171) 724 1751
Fax: (0171) 723 0932
Web Site: www.hopkins.co.uk

Architecture

**Israel Callas Shortridge
Associates**
245 South Robertson
Boulevard
Suite 205
Beverly Hills
Los Angeles CA 90211
USA
Tel: (310) 652 8087
Fax: (310) 652 3383

Architecture

Charles Jencks Architect
19 Lansdowne Walk
Holland Park
London W11
England
Tel: (0171) 727 8216

Architecture

Eva Jiricna Architects
Sun Court House
18–26 Essex Road
London N1 8LN
England
Tel: (0171) 704 7300
Fax: (0171) 226 8903

Architecture

Jan Kaplicky
21C Conduit Place
London WC2 1HS
England
Tel: (0171) 723 4141
Fax: (0171) 723 1131
Web Site:
www.future-systems.com

Architecture

Ben Kelly
10 Stoney Street
London SE1 9AD
England
Tel: (0171) 378 8116
Fax: (0171) 378 8366

Architecture

McBride and Associates
480 Canal Street
New York NY 10013
USA
Tel: (212) 941 0818
Fax: (212) 274 1856

Architecture

Stefano de Martino
Via Conservatorio 20
20122 Milan
Italy
Tel: (02) 7600 2964
Fax: (02) 772 940

Architecture

Rick Mather Architects
123 Camden High Street
London NW1
England
Tel: (0171) 284 1726
Fax: (0171) 267 7826

Architecture

**Munkenbeck + Marshall
Architects**
Exmouth House
3–11 Pine Street
London EC1R 0JH
England
Tel: (0171) 833 1407
Fax: (0171) 837 5416

Architecture

One Off Ltd
See Ron Arad Associates

Outram Cullinan & Co Ltd
65 Kingsway
London WC2 6TD
England
Tel: (0171) 834 7447
Fax: (0171) 828 3349

Architecture

John Pawson
Unit B
70–78 York Way
London N1 9AG
England
Tel: (0171) 837 2929

Architecture

Powell-Tuck Associates
14 Barley Mow Passage
London W4 4PH
England
Tel: (0181) 747 9988
Fax: (0181) 747 8838

Architecture

Richard Rogers Partnership Ltd
Thames Wharf Studio
Rainville Road
London W6 9HA
England
Tel: (0171) 385 1235
Tel: (0171) 385 8409
Web Site:
www.richardrogers.co.uk

Architecture

Michael Russum
Birds, Portchmouth, Russum
9 Hatton Street
London NW8 9PL
England
Tel: (0171) 724 1505
Fax: (0171) 724 0559

Architecture

Charles Rutherfoord
51 The Chase
London SW4 0NP
England
Tel: (0171) 627 0182

Architecture

Claudio Silvestrin
392 St John Street
London EC1V 4NN
England
Tel: (0171) 833 8691
Fax: (0171) 833 1861

Architecture

Stanton Williams
Diespeker Wharf
38 Graham Street
London N1 8JX
England
Tel: (0171) 880 6400
Fax: (0171) 880 6401

Architecture

Von Gerkan, Marg and partner
Elbchaussee 139
Hamburg
Germany
Tel: (40) 88 1500

Architecture

Andreas Weber
Nymphenburgerstrasse 79
Munich
Germany
Tel: (89) 49 75 38

Architecture

David Wild Design & Build
44 Rochester Place
London NW1
England
Tel: (0171) 267 7126

Architecture

John Young Architect
c/o Richard Rogers
Partnership Ltd
Rainville Road
Thames Wharf
London W6 9HA
England
Tel: (0171) 385 1235
Fax: (0171) 385 8409
Web Site:
www.richardrogers.co.uk

Architecture

Index

INDEX

Bibliography

Billcliffe, Roger
Charles Rennie Mackintosh,
The Complete Furniture,
Furniture Drawings and
Interior Designs
John Murray
1979

Calloway, Stephen
The Elements of Style
Mitchell Beazley
1991

Coad, Emma Dent
Spanish Design
and Architecture
Studio Vista
1990

Collins, Michael,
Papadallis, Andreas
Post-Modern Design,
Academy Editions
1989

Glancey, Jonathan
New British Architecture
Thames and Hudson
1989

Glancey, Jonathan
Bryant, Richard
The New Moderns
Mitchell Beazley
1990

Huygen, Frederique
British Design,
Image and Identity
Thames and Hudson
1989

Isaacs, Reginald
Gropius, An Illustrated
Biography of the Creator
of the Bauhaus
Bullfinch
1986

Jencks, Charles
Architecture Today
Academy Editions
1988

Jencks, Charles
The New Moderns
Academy Editions
1990

Julier, Guy
New Spanish Design
Thames and Hudson
1991

Mauries, Patrick
Fornasetti,
Designer of Dreams
Thames and Hudson
1991

Moor, Andrew
Contemporary
Stained Glass
Mitchell Beazley
1989

Neuhart, John and Marilyn
Eames, Ray,
Eames Design,
The Work of the Office of
Charles and Ray Eames
Thames and Hudson
1989

Pasca, Vanni
Vico Magistretti,
Elegance and Innovation
in Postwar Italian Design
Thames and Hudson
1991

Pawley, Martin
Eva Jiricna,
Design in Exile
Fourth Estate
1990

Rogers, Richard
Richard Rogers
and Architects
Academy Editions
1985

Sudjic, Deyan
The Lighting Book
Mitchell Beazley
1985

Sudjic, Deyan
New Directions in
British Architecture,
Norman Foster, Richard
Rogers, James Stirling
Thames and Hudson
1988

Tapert, Annette
Swid Powell
Objects and Architects
Thames and Hudson
1990

Westphal, Uwe
The Bauhaus
Studio Editions
1991

Acknowledgments

Author's acknowledgments

Thank you to Hilu Ginger for her invaluable assistance with research, to Graham Bell for the Directory computer program and to my sons, James and Oliver Niesewand, and my husband, Christopher Ward, for their help and support.

Thank you to all the manufacturers, agents and designers who generously submitted an excellent range of material for selection. Finally, I would like to thank everyone at Mitchell Beazley.